# SPEAKING IBAN

## by
## Burr Baughman

Edited

by

Rev. Dr. James T. Reuteler, Ph.D.

# SPEAKING IBAN

## TABLE OF CONTENTS

# INTRODUCTION

Burr Baughman is deceased, but he meant a lot to our family. When Barbara and I were married, Burr walked down the aisle with Barbara representing her father. We used this book to study the Iban langauge, which we used for eight years. We have come to love the Iban people and their language. We read from the Iban Upper Room and from the Iban Bible. Since we left Sarawak, we have returned only three times, but we hope to return many more times, now that we're retired.

Our copy of *Speaking Iban* has shown its age, and I decided to edit a new copy, mainly four ourselves, but also for anyone who would like to learn the Iban language I have changed very little in Burr's book. Recently while we were in Sarawak, we learned that some of the spelling of Iban words has changed. With our Iban Bible and Hymnbook, I discovered many of those changes. The most significant changes have to do with the elimination of the letter "o" and the replacement of that letter with "u." Beyond the spelling I changed very little.

I kept the main symbol from the earlier book, which was designed by Hasbie Sulaiman. With the use of Photo Shop I was able to bring the symbol back o life, even though I do not know what the symbol means. I do know that it is a typical symbol, similar, but not identical, to those one might see on many of the Iban artifacts. Below is the *Preface* from the original book, published on July 23, 1963:

The Rev. Burr Baughman of The Methodist Church, Kapit, who has lived and worked in Sarawak since 1948 has been preparing a series of Iban language lessons. These lessons are not yet completed, but it is felt that the available material would be of great value to persons wishing to learn Iban and to understand the Iban people better. These words were written by Alastair Morrison of Kuching, Sarawak.

Burr also gave some advice to those of us who would like to speak Iban correctly. Here's what he says:

These lessons are designed for the person who wishes to learn to speak the Iban language. So speak the words and phrases and sentences aloud. Find an Iban teacher or informant who will be able to give you the proper pronunciation of the words and sentences. Have him or her repeat each word, phrase or sentence first. Then you follow carefully the way he or she has said it. Repeat the sentences frequently, to get easily familiar with the sound and rhythm of the words. When you come to exercises with questions and answers, do these orally. Even the sentences for translation should be done orally before they are written.

If your teacher pronounces these words differently from the way in which they are described in these lessons, follow the pronunciation given by the Iban person. This needs to be stressed. People of other languages can know a good deal of Iban. But if you wish to learn Iban properly, you must hear it spoken by an Iban, not by a member of any other group.

Then one further warning is needed here. Frequently when you ask someone to repeat a single word or short phrase, he gives a distorted pronunciation or stress to that word or phrase. This may be partly to emphasize a sound which you are not getting properly. It may be to make the sound of the word fit more closely to what he thinks that word looks like in its printed form. So have your informant use the word in a complete sentence. Usually this will bring out the proper pronunciation.

In going through these lessons, please keep in mind that the language here is based on the dialect most common in the Kapit District of the Third (now the Seventh) Division, Sarawak. Some of the words and expressions, then, are different from commonly used words and expressions in other areas of Sarawak. But the Ibans from all areas of Sarawak speak together and understand each other with no difficulty. And as a general rule, while Ibans may laugh at pronunciations or colloquialisms of another area, they accept such different usages as proper Iban.

Be wary of the spelling, but do not be worried by it. The spelling of Iban has not yet settled down to one accepted standard. The orthography used in these lessons is only one of several common versions. It is only a transition stage, and will be superseded by slightly different forms. If you, however, get the proper sounds of Iban words firmly fixed in mind, you will be able to understand and work out the variant spellings you will meet.

These lessons, of course, are only the barest beginnings in the learning of the Iban language. On that understanding they are going out with my hope that they may be of some value to who are starting to study this language.

I am not the one who should write another book on *Speaking Iban*, but I have studied this book from cover to cover, and I agree with everything Burr has said on learning the Iban language. I have edited his book for myself, and if it can help anyone else who desires to speak Iban, then my purpose in editing Burr Baughman's book, has fulfilled its purpose.

Rev. Dr. James T. Reuteler, P.hD.

Aurora, Colorado

Jim@Reuteler.org

www.Jim.Reuteler.org

# SPEAKING IBAN

## LESSON 1

| | |
|---|---|
| randau | conversation |
| di | at, in, on |
| rumah | house |
| Iban | Iban, Sea Dayak |
| pelajar | lesson |
| jaku | word, statement, saying; language |
| baru | new, fresh |
| tabi' | hello; greetings |
| apai | father; term of address and respect used when speaking to an older man, a superior, or an official. |

Tabi', apai.      Hello, father.

| | |
|---|---|
| anak | child; term of address used to a younger person, male or female |
| duduk | sit, sit down |

Tabi' anak. Duduk, anak.      Hello, son. Sit down, son.

| | |
|---|---|
| tu' | this, these |
| besai | big, large |

Rumah tu' besai. Besai.      This house (is) big. (Yes, it is) big.

| | |
|---|---|
| berapa | how many? how much? |
| pintu | door; a classifier for rooms in a long-house |

Berapa pintu, apai?      How many doors (are there), father?

| | |
|---|---|
| mayuh | much, many, numerous |

Mayuh pintu.      (There are) many doors.

| | |
|---|---|
| sapa | who? what (of a name)? |
| tuai | old; elder, leader |
| Tuai | title of the official leader of the long-house community. |

7

| | | |
|---|---|---|
| Sapa Tuai Rumah? | | Who (is) the Tuai Rumah? |
| | aku | I, my, me |
| Aku Tuai Rumah. | | I (am) the Tuai Rumah. |
| | nuan | you, your (singular); thou, thee, thine; this is a more formal term of respect |
| Besai rumah nuan, apai. | | Your house (is) big, father. |
| | ari | from |
| | ni | which? where? what? |
| | tadi' | just now (past time) |
| Ari ni tadi', anak? | | Where (did you come) from just now, son? |
| | pasar | village, town |
| Ari pasar tadi', apai. | | From the town just now, father. |
| | umai | rice fields, farm |
| Aku ari umai tadi'. | | I (came) from the rice field just now. |
| Besai umai nuan? | | (Are) your rice fields big? |
| Besai. | | (Yes, they are) big. |
| Sapa di umai? | | Who (is) at the farm? |
| Anak aku di umai. | | My children (are) at the farm. |
| Apai aku di rumah. | | My father (is) at the house. |
| | mupuk | make a start |
| Aku mupok, apai. | | I'll make a start, father. |
| | au' | yes, all right |
| Au', mupuk, anak. | | All right, make a start, son. |

## NOTE A:  GLOTTAL STOP

Notice the apostrophe at the ends of the words in the first list of Iban words below. Contrast the pronunciation of the final vowels in these words with the pronunciation of the final vowels in the words without the apostrophe in the second list.

jaku', tu', tadi', au'

baru, aku, ari, di, randau

| | |
|---|---|
| jaku' | baru |
| tu' | aku |
| tabi' | ari |
| tadi' | di |
| au' | randau |

This apostrophe is not used in conventional spelling, but is added in these first lessons to indicate the glottal stop: when the glottal cords are brought tightly together to cut off suddenly any sound. A word with a glottal stop is given its full pronunciation; then the voice comes to a sudden end before carrying on with the next word.

Notice how the single vowel "i" changes in sound almost to "e" before a glottal stop, and the single-vowel "u" changes in sound almost to "o" before the glottal stop.

Thus there is no difference in sound between the final "u" and the final "o" before a glottal stop. (The final vowel sound of these words is the same: Jaku', —tu'.) In the newest spelling, the "o" is changed to "u". Jako becomes Jaku.

There also is often no difference in sound between the final "i" and the final "e" before a glottal stop.

As conventional spelling does not indicate the glottal stop, the student must learn where it applies simply by listening to an Iban speaker, or by looking up relevant words in a dictionary which tells where the glottal stop is used. This situation is confusing, as a new word seen for the first time in writing, and ending with "u" or "i", is ambiguous as to the sound of the final vowel.

Practice pronouncing the following phrases and sentences.

| | |
|---|---|
| Jaku' tu' | This word |
| Jaku' baru tu' | This new word |
| Tu' jaku' baru. | This (is) a new saying. |
| Jaku' aku tadi' jaku baru. | My words just now (were) a new statement. |
| Randau tu | This conversation |
| Au', tu' randau apai tadi'. | Yes, this (was) father's conversation just now. |
| Jaku' aku, tabi'. | My word (was) hello. (i.e. I said hello.) |
| Mayuh jaku' anak tadi'. | Many (were) the words of the child just now. (i.e. The child talked a lot just now.) |

## NOTE B: POSITION OF MODIFIERS

Notice that a word which modifies a noun generally follows that noun.

| | |
|---|---|
| Rumah tu' | This house |
| Rumah baru | New house |
| Rumah besai | Big house |
| Jaku' tu' | This word |
| Jaku' baru | New word |
| Umai tu' | This rice field |
| Umai besai | Big rice field |
| Pasar tu' | This village |
| Pasar besai | Big town |
| Pasar baru | New village. |

Exceptions to this rule are the words which express amount and number.

General words of amount (much, many, few, etc.) may be, and frequently are, placed before the words they modify. There is no hard and fast rule to follow, but in general we may say that usually words of amount precede the words they modify.

| | |
|---|---|
| Mayuh pintu | Many doors |
| Mayuh Anak di rumah. | Many children (are) at the house. |
| Mayuh Iban di umai. | Many Ibans (are) at the rice fields. |

Cardinal numbers (one, two, three, etc.) are placed before the words they directly modify. (See the next lesson)

## NOTE C: POSSESSIVE

One way to indicate the possessive is to put the name of the possessor immediately following the name of the thing possessed.

| | |
|---|---|
| Rumah aku | My house |
| Rumah sapa? | Whose house? |
| Umai nuan | Your rice field |
| Umai Iban | Rice fields of the Ibans |
| Pintu apai | Father's door |
| Pintu Tuai Rumah | The door of the Tuai Rumah |
| Jaku' anak | A child's word |
| Jaku' apai | Father's word |
| Anak sapa? | Whose child? |
| Apai anak | Child's father |

## EXERCISES

### 1. Sentences

Here are some sentences for you to practice. The structures, the patterns, are steady. The words change. It is according to these patterns that Ibans speak. Learn to speak with them along these patterns.

| | |
|---|---|
| Rumah tu' baru. | This house (is) new. |
| Pelajar tu' baru. | This lesson (is) new. |
| Jaku tu' baru. | This saying (is) new. |
| Pintu tu' baru. | This door (is) new. |
| Tuai Rumah tu' baru. | This Tuai Rumah (is) new. |
| Pasar tu' baru. | This village (is) new. |
| Umai tu' baru. | This rice field (is) new. |
| Rumah tu' baru. | This house (is) new. |
| Rumah tu' besai. | This house (is) large. |
| Rumah tu' mayuh. | These houses are numerous. |

| | |
|---|---|
| Tu' rumah baru. | This (is a) new house. |
| Tu' pelajar baru. | This (is a) new lesson. |
| Tu' jaku' baru. | This (is a) new saying. |
| Tu' pintu baru | This (is a) new door. |
| Tu' anak baru. | This (is a) new child. |
| Tu' Tuai Rumah baru. | This Iis a) new Tuai Rumah. |
| Tu' pasar baru. | This (is a) new village. |
| Tu' umai baru. | This (is a) new rice field. |
| | |
| Tu' rumah baru | This (is a) new house. |
| Tu' rumah Iban | This (is an) Iban house. |
| Tu' rumah besai. | This (is a) big house. |
| | |
| Tu' rumah apai. | This (is) father's house. |
| Tu' rumah anak. | This (is) the child's house. |
| Tu' rumah aku. | This (is) my house. |
| Tu' rumah nuan. | This (is) your house. |
| | |
| Aku ari umai tadi'. | I (came) from the rice field just now. |
| Apai ari umai tadi'. | Father (came) from the rice field just now. |
| Anak ari umai tadi'. | The child (came) from the rice field just now. |
| Tuai Rumah ari umai tadi'. | The Tuai Rumah (came) from the rice field just now. |
| | |
| Aku ari umai tadi'. | I (came) from the rice field just now. |
| Aku ari pasar tadi'. | I (came) from the village just now. |
| Aku ari rumah tadi'. | I (came) from the house just now. |
| | |
| Mayuh Iban di pasar. | Many Ibans (are) in town. |
| Mayuh Tuai Rumah di pasar. | Many Tuai Rumah (are) in town. |
| Mayuh anak di pasar. | Many children (are) in town. |
| Mayuh Iban di pasar. | Many Ibans (are) in town. |
| Mayuh Iban di rumah. | Many Ibans (are) at the house. |
| Mayuh Iban di umai. | Many Ibans (are) at the rice fields. |

## 2. Translate the following into English.

Tabi' Tuai Rumah!
Aku ari pasar tadi'.
Anak aku mayuh.
Besai umai anak aku.
Apai aku tuai.
Sapa di rumah nuan?
Apai duduk di rumah, anak di umai.

Besai rumah apai.
Mayuh jaku' apai aku.
Mupuk aku, Tuai Rumah.

## 3. Translate the following into Iban.

I am at the farm.
My house is big.
I have many lessons.
My father sits in the house.
The Tuai Rumah came from town just now.
Is this a new lesson, father?
The Tuai Rumah's children are at the farm.
Who is your father?
How many children do you have, father?
I'll get going, Tuai Rumah.

# LESSON 2

|  |  |
|---|---|
| | nama — name |
| | wai — a term of address used for friends, familiars, equals and inferiors |
| Sapa nama nuan, wai? | What (is) your name, friend? |
| Nama aku Manjah anak Kilat. | My name (is) Manjah anak Kilat. |
| | penghulu — chief: an official title, and a common noun |
| | kita' — you, your (plural) |
| | iya — he, him, his; she, her; it, its |
| Sapa penghulu kita'? | Who (is) your chief? |
| Penghulu Sibat anak Semada. | Penghulu Sibat anak Semada', |
| Tu' iya' | This (is) he. (Here he is). |
| Tabi' Penghulu. | Hello, Penghulu. |
| | de' — you, your (singular); this is a term used for friends, familiars, equals and inferiors |
| Tabi' anak. Ari ni de' tadi'? | Hello, son. Where did you (come) from just now? |
| | ili' — downriver |
| Aku ari ili', ari pasar. | I (came) from downriver, from the village. |
| | ulu — upriver |
| Aku ari ulu tadi'. | I (came) from upriver just now. |
| | dini — Where? at what place? |
| | bilik — family room (of longhouse); also used to denote family |
| Dini bilik nuan, Penghulu? | Where (is) your family room, Penghulu? |
| | nya' — that, those |
| | am — come along |
| | bini — wife |
| | enggau — and, with; to accompany |
| | indai — mother; term of address and respect to an older woman |
| Nya' bilik aku. Am! | That (is) my family room. Come! |
| Tu' bini enggau indai aku. | These (are) my wife and mother. |
| Tabi' wai. Tabi', indai. | Hello, friend. Hello, mother. |

LESSON 2

| | | |
|---|---|---|
| | lelaki | male |
| | indu' | woman; female |
| | anak lelaki | boy, son |
| | anak indu' | girl, daughter |
| Tu' anak lelaki aku. | | These (are) my sons. |
| Tu' anak indu' aku. | | These (are) my daughters |
| | iku' | tail; numeral classifier for living creatures, and for persons (human or spiritual) |
| Berapa iku' anak lelaki Penghulu? | | How many sons (do you have) Penghulu? |
| | dua | two |
| | tiga | three |
| | lima' | five |
| | samua | all |
| Anak lelaki aku dua iku'. | | I have two sons. |
| Anak indu' aku tiga iku'. | | I have three daughters. |
| Samua anak aku lima' iku. | | I have five children altogether. |
| | manuk | fowl, chicken |
| Mayuh manuk Penghulu? | | (Do you Have) many chickens, Penghulu? |
| | puluh | a multiple of ten: used in numbers 10, 20-99 |
| Au' manuk aku dua puluh iku'. | | Yes, I have twenty chickens. |
| Dini manuk nya'? | | Where are those chickens? |
| | baruh | under, beneath, below; low, humble |
| | tinduk | sleep |
| | uduk/ukui | dog |
| | alam/dalam | in, inside |
| Manuk nya' di rumah. | | Those chickens (are) at the house. |
| Manuk tinduk baruh rumah. | | The chickens sleep below the house. |
| Uduk aku tinduk alam rumah. | | My dogs sleep in the house. |

# LESSON 2

## NOTE A: SENTENCE STRUCTURE

### 1. Simple Statement

Subject-Predicate Arrangement
The simplest form of Iban statements is the Subject-Predicate construction, without verb.

Nya' bilik aku.

That (is) my room.
Subject: "Nya'"
Predicate: "bilik aku"

In this type of sentence a verb must be supplied in the English translation to make a proper sentence, but it is not used in the Iban version. Such sentences, when translated into English usually take some form of the verb "to be"; though "to come", "to go" and "to have" are also common.

First of this group are those sentences in which the predicate is a word, phrase or clause that is the equivalent of a noun or pronoun.

Tu' Penghulu aku.　　　　　　This (is) my Penghulu.
Jaku' tu' jaku' baru.　　　　　These words (are) a new statement.
Nama iya Undi anak Panyau.　His name (is) Undi anak Panyau.
Anak Tuai Rumah apai aku.　The son of the Tuai Rumah (is) my father.
Samua anak Penghulu anak indu'. All the Penghulu's children (are) girls.

Next comes that construction in which the predicate acts as the equivalent of an adjective.

Rumah tu' baru.　　　This house (is) new.
Penghulu nya' tuai.　That Penghulu (is) old.
Umai Iban besai,　　Iban farms (are) large.
Kita' Iban mayuh.　You Ibans (are) numerous.
Uduk iya indu'.　　　His dog (is) female.

Another class of verbless predicates in Iban sentences is that in which the predicate acts as the equivalent of a prepositional phrase. In this class the verb supplied in the English translation may be some form of "to come" or "to go" (or word of similar meaning) —with or without adverbial modifiers.

17

(The preposition "ka" is frequently used in this type of sentence, and will be met in the next lesson.)

| | |
|---|---|
| Anak indu' nuan di umai. | Your daughters (are) at the farm. |
| Manok kita' baruh rumah. | Your chickens (are) under the house. |
| Aku ari ili'. | I (came) from downriver. (or: I am from downriver.) |
| Bini aku di rumah apai iya. | My wife (is) at her father's house. |
| Penghulu ari pasar tadi'. | The Penghulu (came) from the village just now. |

Finally we have the construction in which the verbless predicate in an Iban sentence is concerned with numbers and amounts. To translate this type of sentence properly, the English version arranges the sentence, and usually supplies some form of the verb "to have".

| | |
|---|---|
| Anak lelaki aku dua iku'. | I have two sons. (My sons two tail.) |
| Manuk iya dua puluh lima' iku'. | He has twenty-five chickens. (His chickens twenty-five tail.) |
| Samua uduk iya tiga iku'. | He has three dogs altogether. (All his dogs three tail.) |
| Manuk apai aku mayuh. | MY father has many chickens. (My father's chickens many.) |
| Anak indu' Penghulu tiga iku'. | The Penghulu has three daughters. (The Penghulu's daughters three tail.) |

(As more numeral classifiers—see Note B below— and words of measure are learned, the student will be able to add further examples).

Note, then, that the following types of statements do not take verbs in Iban, unless it is desired to emphasize the action or condition which would be expressed by the verbs:

(i) simple statements requiring some form of the verb "to be" in the English version

(ii) simple statements of proceeding to or from some location

The next large classification of simple subject-predicate sentences is that group in which the predicate is introduced by a verb.

| | |
|---|---|
| Manuk tinduk baruh rumah.. | Chickens sleep beneath the house. |
| Penghulu duduk di bilik. | The Penghulu is sitting in the room. |
| Mayuh Iban mupuk tadi'. | Many Ibans made a start just now. |
| Samua indu' tinduk di bilik. | All the women are sleeping in the room. |

**Predicate-Subject Arrangement**

(a) **Without Verb.** A very common type of Iban sentence is a statement expressed in what is translated into English as a simple predicate-subject construction.

| | |
|---|---|
| Bilik aku nya'. | This (is) my room. (My room that.) |

Predicate: "Bilik aku"
Subject: "nya"

This construction type parallels the subject-predicate arrangement just studied. So it may be said that any statement which can be expressed with the verbless subject-predicate construction may also be expressed with the inversion of that construction in the predicate-subject arrangement.

When speaking sentences of this type, it is important to make a slight pause between predicate and subject, to ensure proper comprehension.

| | |
|---|---|
| Penghulu aku tu'. | This (is) my Penghulu. |
| Jaku' baru jaku' tu'. | These words are a new statement. |
| Baru rumah tu'. | This house (is) new. |
| Tuai Penghulu nya'. | That Penghulu (is) old. |
| Mayuh kita' Iban. | You Ibans (are) numerous. |
| Ari Pasar tadi' Penghulu. | The Penghulu (came) from the village just now. |
| Di rumah apai iya bini aku. | My wife (is) at her father's house. |
| Dua iku' anak lelaki aku. | I have two sons. |
| Dua puluh lima' iku' manuk iya. | He has twenty-five chickens. |
| Tiga iku' samua uduk iya. | He has three dogs altogether. |

One reason for placing the predicate first is to give an answer to a specific question.

| | |
|---|---|
| Penghulu nya' tuai? | (Is) that Penghulu old? |
| Tuai Penghulu nya'. | Old he is. |
| Penghulu sapa tu'? | Whose Penghulu (is) this? |
| Penghulu aku tu'. | This (is) my Penghulu. |
| Dini bini nuan? | Where (is) your wife? |
| Di rumah apai iya bini aku. | My wife (is) at her father's house. |
| Berapa iku', anak lelaki nuan? | How many sons do you have? |
| Dua iku' anak lelaki aku. | I have two sons. |

Another reason the predicate may be placed before the subject is to give special emphasis to what is expressed in the predicate. This is particularly true when the predicate is the equivalent of an adjective.

| | |
|---|---|
| Penghulu aku tu'. | (1) This (is) MY Penghulu. |
| | This (is) my PENGHULU. |
| Jaku' baru jaku' tu'. | (2) These words (are) a NEW statement. |
| Anak indu' samua anak Penghulu. | (3) All the Penghulu's children (are) GIRLS. (3) |
| Tuai Penghulu nya'. | (4) That Penghulu (is) OLD. (i.e. very old) |
| Mayuh kita' Iban. | (5) You Ibans (are) numerous (i.e. very numerous) |
| Besai umai Iban. | (6) Iban farms (are) LARGE. (i.e. very large) |
| Ari ili' aku. | (7) I (came) from DOWNRIVER. |
| Di umai anak indu nuan. | (8) Your daughter (is) at the FARM. (8) |
| Dua iku' anak lelaki aku. | (9) I have TWO sons. (9) |
| Tiga iku' anak indu Penghulu. | (10) The Penghulu has THREE daughters. |

In saying this type of verbless, predicate-subject sentence, voice intonation, stress and pause are important. The words of the predicate should be spoken with a rising intonation-special stress may be added if desired; then there must be a definite break, or pause; following which, the words of the subject are spoken with a lower intonation.

For example, with a generally even intonation throughout the sentence, (3) above would mean, "the daughters of all the Penghulu's children"; (5) would mean, "Many of you Ibans"; (8) would mean, "at your daughter's rice field"; and (9) would mean, "two of my sons".

20

(b) **With Verb**. Inversion in a simple sentence with a verb introducing the predicate may be done in either of two ways: by merely placing the verb before its subject; or by placing the entire predicate, including the verb, before the subject.

At this stage of our study we shall look at only the first of these two.

| | |
|---|---|
| Tinduk manuk nya' baruh rumah. | The chickens are sleeping beneath the house. |
| Duduk Penghulu di bilik. | The Penghulu is sitting in the room. |
| Tinduk samua indu' di bilik. | All the women in the room are sleeping. |

Two reasons for the inverted order of verb-subject are those mentioned above: to give an answer to a specific question, and to emphasize what is expressed by the verb.

A third reason for putting the verb before the subject is to express a command, entreaty or exhortation.

With the appropriate intonation of voice, the following indicate command or exhortation.

| | |
|---|---|
| Duduk, wai! | Sit down, friend! |
| Duduk, de'! | Sit down! |
| Tinduk, kita', di bilik. | Sleep in the room. |
| Tinduk samua indu' nya' di bilik. | May all those women in the room sleep! |

Intonation and break are important in the saying of this kind of sentence. The verb must be spoken with a rising, high intonation, followed by a slight break. Then the subject is spoken with a lower intonation, followed by another break. The rest of the sentence follows at still lower intonation until the full stop at the end.

## 2. Simple Question

So far in these lessons we have met questions made up in two ways:

(a) Questions indicated by the use of interrogative words:

| Who? | which? | where? |
|------|--------|--------|
| what? | how much? | how many? |

Here the interrogative word is the first word, or in the first phrase of the sentence. This interrogative word clearly indicates that the sentence is a question, and there can be no doubt of the purpose of the construction.

| Sapa nama de', wai? | What (is) your name, friend? |
|---|---|
| Dini Penghulu kita'? | Where (is) your chief? |
| Berapa iku manuk nuan, indai? | How many chickens (do) you (have), mother? |
| Ari ni anak de' tadi'? | Where (did) your child (come) from just now? |
| Anak ni ari ulu tadi'? | Which child (came) from upriver just now? |

(b) Questions indicated merely by the intonation of the voice.

This type is also quite frequent. As there is no specific word to indicate the question, interrogation must be shown by the rising inflection of the voice, just as in English.

| Besai umai nuan? | (Is) your farm large? |
|---|---|
| Mayuh manuk Penghulu? | (Do you), Penghulu (have) many chickens? |
| Jaku pelajar tu' jaku' baru? | (Are) the words of this lesson new words? |
| Apai nuan tuai? | (Is) your father old? |
| Bini nuan di rumah tadi'? | (Was) your wife at the house just now? |

## NOTE B: NUMERAL CLASSIFIERS

Cardinal numbers in Iban, when used as adjectives to qualify nouns, normally take numeral classifiers. These latter are standardized words which come immediately following the number. Each noun which indicates a concrete object (and some which indicate more intangible things) has a numeral classifier which must be used when the noun is modified by a cardinal number.

Each numeral classifier has a class of nouns with which it is to be used. Each such classifier is a word with its own particular meaning; and it is this relevant meaning which has led to the use of the word in conjunction with other nouns when a cardinal number is involved. It is by context alone that we determine whether a specific word is used as a noun or a numeral classifier.

When a word is used as a numeral classifier it is not normally translated into an English equivalent (except in the possible expression: "_____head of cattle").

In this lesson we have one of the most frequently used of the numeral classifiers: "Iku'", which is used in connection with all living creatures, and with persons, human or spiritual.

| | |
|---|---|
| Lima' iku' manuk baruh rumah. | Five chickens (are) under the house. |
| Tiga iku' Penghulu ari ili' tadi'. | Three chiefs (came) from downriver just now. |
| Dua puluh iku' anak di rumah. | Twenty children (are) at the house. |
| Samua manuk aku lima' puluh tiga iku'. | All my chickens (are) fifty-three. (I have fifty three chickens altogether.) |
| Tu' Tuai Rumah dua iku' ari ulu. | These (are) two Tuai Rumahs from upriver. |
| Berapa iku' anak de', wai? | How many children do you have, friend? |
| Tiga iku', wai. | Three, friend. |

The following general statements, then, may be made concerning the use of numeral classifiers.

1. Every cardinal number modifying a noun which names an object must be followed by a numeral classifier.

2. The cardinal classifier follows immediately after the cardinal number.

3. The noun may either follow the numeral classifier, or come somewhere before the number phrase in the sentence.

4.  In a question using "berapa" ("now many." "how much"), the numeral classifier must be used in conjunction with any noun which names an object.

## NOTE C: TERMS OF ADDRESS

"Wai" is a general term of address, in familiar tone, to anyone more or less on your social level. It may be used to either male or female, young or old—except that a small child would only be addressed thus by an adult facetiously.

It is not proper to use this term when speaking formally to an individual or group, when speaking to an official in his official capacity, or when speaking to a person of higher social or official rank.

The word "wai" is used only in address, never as the subject or object of a verb or other part of speech.

"Penghulu" is the term of address used for men who hold the official rank of Penghulu, or chief. Care should be taken to use this title of honor with all chiefs at all times, and not to offend them with the too-familiar "wai", or "de'."

In general the following may be said concerning terms of address.

1.  When speaking to a person do not frequently use his or her name.

2.  Pronouns are a proper term of address.
    a.  "kita," to more than one
    b.  "nuan," as the polite term for an individual
    c.  "de'," a more familiar, though not impolite, term to an individual of our own general station in life.

3.  When addressing an official, his official title should be used (e.g. "Tuai Rumah," Penghulu," "District Officer"), If the title is expressed with a word in the Iban or other local languages, use that word. If the high official is designated with an English title, use that, and prefix it with the word "tuan" ("Mr.").

4. Rather than constantly using the name of the person addressed, or a pronoun, it is better to use one of the terms of friendship or respect: "wai, apai, indai", and the like.

5. Ibans frequently use kinship terms as terms of address when speaking to relatives. Such kinship terms will be met later in these lessons.

## NOTE D: NOTATION OF NAMES

An Iban name is written thus:

| | | |
|---|---|---|
| Manjah anak Kilat | "Manjah" | Given Name |
| | "anak" | child (son or daughter) of |
| | "Kilat" | father's name |
| Tuai Rumah Kudi anak Sabang | "Tuai Rumah" | Title |
| | "Kudi" | given name |
| | "anak" | child of |
| | "Sabang" | father's name |

A father's title of Tuai Rumah would not normally be recorded in the son's name.

| | | |
|---|---|---|
| Penghulu Sibat anak Penghulu Semada' | "Penghulu" | title |
| Penghulu Sibat anak P, Semada' | "Sibat" | given name |
| P. Sibat anak P. Semada' | "anak" | child of |
| | "Penghulu" | father's title |
| | "Semada'" | father's name |

The name of Penghulu Sibat's son is written like this:

| | | |
|---|---|---|
| Nuak anak Penghulu Sibat | "Nuak" | given name |
| Nuak anak P. Sibat | "anak" | child of |
| | "Penghulu" | father's title |
| | "Sibat" | father's name |

In writing, it is becoming more common to use the father's title of "Penghulu" in recording a name. Frequently, however, the father's title is omitted when speaking the son's name.

The abbreviations "P." and "T.Rh." are acceptable, but not in more formal usage.

## NOTE E: WORDS: pasar, indu', lelaki

"Pasar" comes from a foreign word meaning "marketplace." In Malay, and in the English "bazaar" it is used in this sense.

In Iban, however, "pasar" means "village, town". It is used also in the Iban equivalent of the English expression, "I am going to town;" as meaning going to the shopping, or built-up area of the village or town.

"Indu'" is a word with several meanings. In the first place, as a noun, it means "woman." By extension, it means also "wife"—but only in familiar, or coarse and impolite usage. A man may familiarly and properly speak of his wife in terms of his "woman." A third person so speaking of her is using a term which is familiar, or ranging from uncouth to downright rude; depending on their respective social ranking, or kinship. It is never polite to address a woman as "Indu'."

| | |
|---|---|
| Mayuh indu' di pasar. | Many women (are) in the village. |
| Tu' indu' aku. | This (is) my wife. (Familiar, but correct). |

As an adjective, "Indu'" means female and is placed immediately following the noun it modifies.

It may be used in connection with any living thing which is female in sex.

| | |
|---|---|
| Tu' anak indu ali. | This (is) my daughter. |
| Dua iku' uduk indu di umai. | Two female dogs (are) at the farm. |
| Manuk indu' iya lima' iku'. | He has five hens. |

A less frequent usage translates "indu'" as the "main part," "chief unit," or "center or source" of something.

"Lelaki" is often pronounced with a prolonged "l...." rather than with the "lel...." It is an adjective, meaning "male," but is also used as a noun. It may be used with any living thing which is male in sex.

| | |
|---|---|
| Tu' anak lelaki aku. | This (is) my son. |
| Dua iku' uduk lelaki di umai. | Two male dogs (are) at the farm. |
| Manuk lelaki iya lima' iku'. | He has five cocks. |

## NOTE F. WORD DRILL

We have noticed and practiced the pronunciation of Iban words with the glottal stop. Here is a further drill.

| | |
|---|---|
| Kita', nya', de', ili', iku', indu' | with glottal stop |
| nama, iya, bini, dini, ulu, baru | without glottal stop |

| | |
|---|---|
| kita' | nama |
| nya' | iya |
| de' | dini |
| ili' | bini |
| iku' | ulu |
| indu' | baru |

| | |
|---|---|
| Sapa nama indu' tu'? | What (is) the name of this woman? |
| Dini indu' nya', bini de'? | Where (is) that woman, your wife? |
| Lima' iku' indu' ari ili' tadi'. | Five women (came) from downriver just now. |
| Tiga iku' kita' enggau aku. | Three of you accompany me. |
| Penghulu kita' ari ulu tadi'. | Your Penghulu (came) from upriver just now. |

Now we should notice the pronunciation of words ending in "h" and in "k."

When an Iban word ends in "h," it must be aspirated at the end.

Vowel sound before final "h."

"ah';" does not change.

rumah, mayuh, puluh, baruh

Note that a final "ih" and a final "ch" are practically identical as to sound. A final "oh" and a final "uh" are also practically identical in sound.

Vowel sounds before final "k;"

"ak": no change
"ik": the "i" is pronounced with a brief central glide very similar to the glide expressed by the letter "a" in the Scottish name "Ian."
"ok": the "o" is pronounced with the same type of brief central glide.

It may be noted that this glide is a feature of traditional Iban pronunciation, and is beginning to disappear in modern usage and pronunciation.

anak, bilik, duduk, tinduk, uduk, manuk, mupuk

Contrast the pronunciation of the final syllables of the following list of words.

sapa rumah nya' anak
bini (benih) ili' bilik
baru baruh indu' tinduk
ulu puluh iku' uduk

Now try these sentences.

| | |
|---|---|
| Mayuh manuk baruh rumah. | Many chickens (are) under the house. |
| Anak alam bilik dua puluh iku'. | The children in the room (are) twenty in number. |
| Am, mupuk kitai. | Come, let's start. |
| Uduk mayuh duduk di bilik. | Many dogs sit in the room. |
| Manuk mayuh tinduk baruh bilik. | Many chickens sleep below the room. |

### EXERCISES

#### 1. Sentences

Review the pattern sentences given in the previous lesson. In those patterns substitute new words learned in this second lesson.

| | |
|---|---|
| Sapa nama anak nya'? | What (is the) name of that child? |
| Sapa nama Iban nya'? | What (is the) name of that Iban? |
| Sapa nama Tuai Rumah nya'? | What (is the) name of that Tuai Rumah? |
| Sapa nama lelaki nya'? | What (is the) name of that man? |
| Sapa nama anak lelaki nya'? | What (is the) name of that boy? |
| Sapa nama Penghulu nya'? | What (is the) name of that Penghulu? |
| Sapa nama indu' nya'? | What (is the) name of that woman? |
| Sapa nama anak indu' nya'? | What (is the) name of that girl? |
| Sapa nama anak nuan? | What (is the) name of your child? |
| Sapa nama anak Tuai Rumah? | What (is the) name of the Tuai Rumah's child? |
| Sapa nama anak Penghulu? | What (is the) name of the Penghulu's child? |
| Sapa nama anak kita? | What (are the) names of your children? |
| Sapa nama anak iya? | What (is the) name of his child? |
| Sapa nama anak de'? | What (is the) name of your child? |

| | |
|---|---|
| Dini apai? | Where (is) father? |
| Dini anak? | Where (are the) children? |
| Dini Tuai Rumah? | Where (is the) Tuai Rumah? |
| Dini umai? | Where (is the) farm? |
| Dini Penghulu? | Where (is the) Penghulu? |
| Dini indai? | Where (is) mother? |
| Dini pasar? | Where (is the) village? |
| Dini iya? | Where (is) he? |
| Dini bilik de'? | Where (is) your room? |
| Dini rumah kita'? | Where (is) your house? |
| Dini bini Penghulu? | Where (is the) wife of the Penghulu? |
| Dini anak lelaki nuan? | Where (is) your son? |
| Dini manuk apai? | Where (are) father's chickens? |
| | |
| Iban tinduk di bilik. | Ibans are sleeping in the room. |
| Apai tinduk di bilik. | Father is sleeping in the room. |
| Anak tinduk di bilik. | The children are sleeping in the room. |
| Sapa tinduk di bilik? | Who is sleeping in the room? |
| Aku tinduk di bilik. | I sleep in the room. |
| Indu' tinduk di bilik. | The women are sleeping in the room. |
| | |
| Pengulu tinduk di bilik. | The Pengulu is sleeping in the room. |
| Iya tinduk di bilik. | He is sleeping in the room. |
| Tuai Rumah tinduk di bilik. | The Tuai Rumah is sleeping in the room. |
| De' tinduk di bilik. | You sleep in the room. |
| Indai tinduk di bilik. | Mother sleeps in the room. |
| Anak lelaki nuan tinduk di bilik. | Your son is sleeping in the room. |
| Anak indu' kita' tinduk di bilik. | Your daughters are sleeping in the room. |
| Uduk nya' tinduk di bilik. | Those dogs are sleeping in the room. |
| Samua indu' tinduk di bilik. | All the women are sleeping in the room. |
| | |
| Iban duduk di bilik. | Ibans are sitting in the room. |
| Apai duduk di bilik. | Father is sitting in the room. |
| Anak duduk di bilik. | The children are sitting in the room. |
| Sapa duduk di bilik? | Who is sitting in the room. |
| Aku duduk di bilik. | I am sitting in the room. |
| Indu' duduk di bilik. | The women are sitting in the room. |
| Penghulu duduk di bilik. | The Penghulu is sitting in the room. |
| Iya duduk di bilik. | He is sitting in the room. |
| Tuai Rumah duduk di bilik. | The Tuai Rumah is sitting in the room. |
| De' duduk di bilik. | You are sitting in the room. |
| Indai duduk di bilik. | Mother is sitting in the room. |
| Anak lelaki nuan duduk di bilik. | Your son is sitting in the room. |
| Anak indu' kita duduk di bilik. | Your daughers are sitting in the room. |

| | |
|---|---|
| Uduk nya' duduk di bilik. | Those dogs are sitting in the room. |
| Samua indu' duduk di bilik. | All the women are sitting in the room. |
| | |
| Mayuh Iban di rumah. | Many Ibans (are) at the house. |
| Mayuh Iban di pasar. | Many Ibans (are) in town. |
| Mayuh Iban di umai. | Many Ibans (are) at the rice fields. |
| Mayuh Iban di ili'. | Many Ibans (are) upriver. |

**2. Answer, in Iban, the following questions.**

Sapa nama apai nuan?
Dini rumah nuan?
Dini uduk tinduk di rumah Iban?
Dini manuk tinduk?
Sapa nama Penghulu alam pelajar tu' tadi'? Sibat anak Semada
Berapa iku' anak Penghulu nya'?
Dini bini iya tadi'?
Berapa iku' manuk Penghulu?

**3. Translate the following into English**

Rumah Penghulu rumah besai, mayuh pintu. Rumah nya' di ulu. Indai enggau anak Penghulu di rumah iya. Indai nya' tuai. Bini Penghulu di umai di ila'. Di umai uduk tuai dua iku'. Anak uduk nya' tiga iku'. Manuk Penghulu lima' puluh dua iku' di ulu. Manuk nya' tinduk baruh rumah. Anak manuk nya' alam rumah.

**4. Translate the following into Iban**

Who is your Tuai Rumah? Where does he live? My wife's Tuai Rumah is in this house. He is a big Iban. He has many chickens and dogs. He has five daughters. His daughters are at his farm. His farm is big. He has thirty five chickens. All his chickens are at this house.

Kami Iban duduk di tikai,
    tinduk di tikai.

We Ibans sit on mats,
    and sleep on mats.

| | |
|---|---|
| ngaga' | make, construct, build, do |

Sapa ngaga' tikai nya'?

Who makes those mats?

| | |
|---|---|
| sida' | They, their, them |
| pandai | clever, skillful, expert, good at doing something |
| badas | good, fine, excellent, well, pretty |

Sida' indu' ngaga' tikai.
Indai aku pandai ngaga'.
Iya ngaga' tikai badas.

The (they) women make mats.
My mother is clever at making them.
She makes good mats.

| | |
|---|---|
| sigi' | really, truly; one—of fruit, eggs, or other small objects (i.e. — "Sa" — one plus "igi'" — numeral classifier for these objects) |

Kita' Iban sigi' pandai.
KIta' pandai ngaga' mayuh utai.

You Ibans are really skillful.
You are good at making many things.

| | |
|---|---|
| nemu | know, understand, know how |
| kereja | work, labor |
| kampung | jungle, forest |
| meh | a particle used in sentences for emphasis, for euphony, to indicate some grammatical construction (e.g. imperative), to separate words which together would confuse the meaning of the sentence. |
| pengidup | livelihood, living |

Kami Iban sigi' nemu kereja umai.
Kami nemu kereja kampung.
Nya' meh pengidup kami.

We Ibans do (really) know farm work.
We know jungle work.
This is our living.

| | |
|---|---|
| meri' | give, donate |
| padi | growing rice, rice plants, rice grain in the husk |
| engkayu' | any food eaten with rice |
| keresa | goods, articles, possessions, tools, furniture, equipment |
| nyamai | pleasant, delicious, tasty, comfortable, easy |

| | |
|---|---|
| Kereja umai meri' kita padi. | Farm work gives you rice. |
| Kereja kampung meri' kita' engkayu enggau keresa mayuh. | Jungle work gives you other food and many articles. |
| Kati nyamai engkayu' kampung? | Is jungle food good (delicious)? |

| | |
|---|---|
| makai | eat, consume, devour |
| kitai | we, our, us (inclusive) |
| ka | to, towards |

| | |
|---|---|
| Au', nyamai, Am, makai kitai. | Yes, good. Come along. Let's eat. |
| Ka bilik meh kitai. | Let's go to the room. |
| Kitai makai engkayu' kampung. | We'll eat some jungle food. |

## NOTE A: PARENTHESES IN TRANSLATIONS

Beginning with this lesson, parentheses have been omitted in writing ordinary translations of Iban sentences.

No translation from one language to another can be a direct one-for-one, or word-for-word translation. Any translation must aim, rather, at getting across the idea of the original: by using equivalent words as far as possible; and by making clear the relations between various elements of the original speech or writing—though not necessarily by using the same types of construction.

Thus any translation includes words for which there are no exact equivalents in the original, and omits words which are in the original, but for which no equivalents exist in the translation language, or which are not necessary in the grammatical forms used in the translation. Furthermore, of course, each language has its own preferred order of words. In any good translation the order of words is often different from the order in the original.

**Word-For-Word**

Nya' tikai.
Bisi' mayuh tikai di rumah Iban?
Kati samua tikai kita' besai?

That mat.
Are many mats at house Iban?
All mats your big?

**Idiomatic, with Parenthesees**

That (is a) mat.
(There) are many mats in (an) Iban
house.
(Are) all our mats large?

**Idiomatic, without Parentheses**

That is a mat.
There are many mats in an Iban
house.
Are all your mats large?

This latter form will be used in these lessons from now on. Material in parentheses will be used only when the idiomatic translation seems so different from the original as to warrant some explanation.

## NOTE B: VERBS

This third lesson is to provide practice in the use of simple verbs.

So far in these lessons you have met the following words which have been used as verbs. Practice their pronunciation.

| | |
|---|---|
| am | come along |
| bisi' | there is, there are; to be; to have |
| duduk | to sit |
| makai | to eat |
| meda' | to see |
| meri' | to give |
| mupuk | To make a start |
| nadai | There is not |
| nemu | to know |
| ngaga' | to make |
| tinduk | to sleep |

33

1. Most of these may be used with the subject preceding the verb. Use this order, subject-before-verb, for all ordinary purposes of a simple statement.

| | |
|---|---|
| Penghulu bisi' tiga iku' anak indu'. | The Penghulu has three daughters. |
| Apai duduk di ruai. | Father is sitting on the veranda. |
| Anak nya' makai engkayu' nyamai nya. | Those children eat that tasty food. |
| Sida' meda' uduk mit. | They see a small dog. |
| Indai meri' anak iya engkayu' nyamai. | The mother gives her child tasty food. |
| | |
| Kami mupuk. | We are making a start. |
| Indu' nya' nadai anak. | That woman has no children. |
| Anak nemu pelajar sida'. | The children know their lesson. |
| Iban ngaga' ruai besai. | Ibans make big verandas. |
| Anak tinduk di bilik. | The child is sleeping in the room. |

2. Most of these verbs may also be used with the subject following the verb. This order, verb-before-subject, is used when you wish to emphasize the action of the verb.

| | |
|---|---|
| Am kitai. | Let's go. |
| Ka ruai meh kitai, wai. | To the veranda with us, friends. |
| Duduk sida' di ruai. | They are sitting on the veranda. |
| Makai anak nya' di bilik. | Those children are eating in the room. |
| | |
| Meda' aku! | I see! |
| Mupuk kitai. | We're making a start, or Let's make a start. |
| | |
| Nemu sida' anak jaku' tu'. | Those children know these words. |

3. Of the verbs already given, only the following forms may be used in the equivalent of the imperative. (A later lesson will explain this.)

| | |
|---|---|
| duduk | Sit! |
| tinduk | Sleep! |

## NOTE C: "BISI'," "NADAI"

"Bisi'" has the basic meaning of "there is," or "there are" (present, past, or future time).

Whenever "bisi'" is used with no noun or pronoun as subject, it has this basic meaning.

| | |
|---|---|
| Bisi' manuk baruh rumah. | There are chickens beneath the house. |
| Bisi' mayuh uduk. | There are many dogs. |
| Bisi' indu' di bilik. | There is a woman in the room. |
| Bisi' pasar besai di ili. | There is a big town downriver. |
| Bisi' tiga iku' anak lelaki di umai. | There are three boys at the farm. |

Note that the context alone can show whether "bisi'" is singular or plural. If there is no clue in the context, "bisi'" may be translated into English in either the singular or plural form.

A further meaning of "bisi'" is "there are some:" or just "some." This is seen where related but contrasting statements are made, each introduced by "bisi'."

| | |
|---|---|
| Bisi' rumah besai. | Some houses are big. |
| Bisi' rumah mit. | Some houses are small. |
| Bisi' Iban di ruai. | Some Ibans are on the veranda. |
| Bisi' Iban di bilik. | Some Ibans are in the room. |
| Bisi' manuk baruh rumah. | Some chickens are beneath the house. |
| Bisi' manuk alam rumah. | Some chickens are in the house. |
| Bisi' anak tinduk. | Some children are sleeping. |
| Bisi' anak makai. | Some children are eating. |
| Bisi' kita' ari ulu? | Some of you are from upriver? |
| Bisi' kita' ari ili'. | Some of you are from downriver. |

"Bisi'" can also mean "to have." When used thus, a special subject is mentioned for the verb.

| | |
|---|---|
| Aku bisi' dua iku uduk. | I have two dogs. |
| Penghulu bisi' lima' iku' anak. | The Penghulu has five children. |
| Kami bisi' mayuh padi. | We have much (unhusked) rice. |
| Indai Tuai Rumah bisi' tikai badas. | The mother of the Tuai Rumah has a good mat. |
| Apai bisi' engkayu' nyamai. | Father has some tasty food (with his rice). |

"Nadai" has the basic meaning of "there is not," or "there are not" (present, past or future time).

Whenever "nadai" is used with no noun or pronoun as subject, it has this basic meaning.

| | |
|---|---|
| Nadai manuk baruh rumah. | There are no chickens beneath the house. |
| Nadai mayuh uduk. | There are not many dogs. |
| Nadai indu' di bilik. | There are no women in the room. |
| Nadai pasar besai di ili'. | There is no large town downriver. |
| Nadai anak lelaki di umai. | There are no boys at the farm. |

As with "bisi'," the context alone can show whether "nadai" is singular or plural. If there is no clue in the context, "nadai" may be translated into English in either the singular or plural form.

"Nadai" also means "to have not." When used thus, a specific subject is used with the verb.

| | |
|---|---|
| Aku nadai uduk. | I have no dogs. |
| Penghulu nadai anak. | The Penghulu has no children. |
| Kami nadai mayuh padi. | We do not have much unhusked rice. |
| Indai Tuai Rumah nadai tikai badas. | The mother of the Tuai Rumah does not have any good mats. |
| Apai nadai engkayu' nyamai. | Father does not have any tasty food with his rice. |

## NOTE D: "KAMI," "KITAI"

"Kami" and "kitai" are the first person plural, personal pronouns.

A speaker using "kami" means the "we" which does not include the person or persons to whom he or she is talking.

| | |
|---|---|
| Kami nadai padi. | We have no unhusked rice. |
| Kita' bisi' mayuh padi. | You have much rice. |
| Kami lelaki tinduk di ruai. | We men sleep on the veranda. |
| Kita' indu' tinduk di bilik. | You women sleep in the room. |
| Tu' engkayu' kita'. | This is your food. |
| Nya engkayu' kami. | This is ours. |

A speaker using "kitai'" means the "we" which includes the person or persons to whom he or she is talking.

| | |
|---|---|
| Am, wai ka pasar kitai. | Come along, friends. Let's go to town. |
| Kitai bisi' Penghulu badas. | We have a good Penghulu. |
| Kita' bisi' dua iku' uduk. | You have two dogs. |
| Aku bisi' tiga iku'. | I have three dogs. |
| Samua uduk kitai lima' iku'. | We have five dogs altogether. |

## NOTE E: PRONOUN PLUS NOUN

"Kami Iban" means "we Ibans." This English construction is familiar to you, so the parallel Iban phrase need cause no trouble.

Similarly, "sida' Iban" means "they Ibans." This is not an accepted English phrase, but the Iban phrase is common, and frequently used. It may be translated into idiomatic English as, "the Ibans," or "those Ibans."

## EXERCISES

### Sentences

Review the sentences given in previous lessons. In those patterns substitute new words leaned in this lesson.

Here are more sentences for you to practice.

| | |
|---|---|
| Bisi' tikai di rumah. | There are mats at the house. |
| Bisi' Iban di rumah. | There are Ibans at the house. |
| Bisi' anak di rumah. | There are children at the house. |
| Bisi' uduk di rumah. | There are dogs at the house. |
| Bisi' keresa di rumah. | There is furniture at the house. |
| Bisi' indu' di rumah. | There are women at the house. |
| Bisi' manuk di rumah. | There are chickens at the house. |
| Bisi' padi di rumah. | There is rice at the house. |
| | |
| Bisi' Iban di pasar. | There are Ibans in the village. |
| Bisi' Iban di bilik. | There are Ibans in the room. |
| Bisi' Iban di kampung. | There are Ibans in the jungle. |
| Bisi' Iban di umai. | There are Ibans iat the farm. |
| Bisi' Iban di ruai. | There are Ibans on the veranda. |

Nadai tikai du rumah,
Nadai Iban di rumah,
Nadai anak di rumah.
Nadai uduk di rumah.
Nadai keresa di rumah.
Nadai indu' di rumah.
Nadai manuk di rumah.
Nadai padi di rumah.

There are no mats at the house.
There are no Ibans at the house.
There are no children at the house.
There are no dogs at the house.
There is no furniture at the house.
There are no women at the house.
There are no chickens at the house.
There is no rice at the house.

Nadai Iban di pasar.
Nadai Iban di bilik.
Nadai Iban di kampung.
Nadai Iban di umai.
Nadai Iban di ruai.

There are no Ibans at the village.
There are no Ibans in the room.
There are no Ibans in the jungle.
There are no Ibans at the farm.
There are no Ibans on the veranda.

Aku bisi' anak.
Kita' bisi' anak.
De' bisi' anak.
Sida' bisi' anak.
Nuan bisi' anak.
Iya bisi' anak.
Kami bisi' anak.
Kitai bisi' anak.

I have children.
You have children.
You have children.
They have children.
You have children.
He or she has children.
We have children.
We have children.

Aku bisi' padi.
Aku bisi' uduk.
Aku bisi' keresa.
Aku bisi' anak indu'.
Aku bisi' anak lelaki.
Aku bisi' manuk.
Aku bisi' tikai.
Aku bisi' engkayu.

I have unhusked rice.
I have dogs.
I have furniture.
I have daughters
I have sons.
I have chickens.
I have mats.
I have food to eat with rice.

Aku nadai anak.
Kita' nadai anak.
De' nadai anak.
Sida' nadai anak.
Nuan nadai anak.
Iya nadai anak.
Kami nadai anak.
Kitai nadai anak.

I have no children.
You have no children.
You have no children.
They have no children.
You have no children.
He or she has no children.
We have no children.
We have no children.

| | |
|---|---|
| Iya nadai padi | He or she has no unhusked rice. |
| Iya nadai uduk. | He or she has no dogs. |
| Iya nadai keresa. | He or she has no furniture. |
| Iya nadai anak indu'. | He or she has no daughters. |
| Iya nadai anak lelaki. | He or she has no sons. |
| Iya nadai manuk. | He or she has no chickens. |
| Iya nadai tikai. | He or she has no mats. |
| Iya nadai engkayu'. | He or she has nothing to eat with rice. |
| | |
| Sida' meda' Penghulu nya'. | They see that Penghulu. |
| Iya meda' Penghulu nya'. | He or she sees that Penghulu. |
| Aku meda' Penghulu nya'. | I see that Penghulu. |
| Kita' meda' Penghulu nya'. | You see that Penghulu. |
| Nuan meda' Penghulu nya'. | You see that Penghulu. |
| Kitai meda' Penghulu nya'. | We see that Penghulu. |
| De' meda' Penghulu nya'. | You see that Penghulu. |
| Kami meda' Penghulu nya'. | We see that Penghulu. |
| Sida' meda' rumah nya'. | They see that house. |
| Sida' meda' anak nya'. | They see that child. |
| Sida meda' indu' nya'. | They see that woman. |
| | |
| Sida' meda' uduk nya'. | They see that dog. |
| Sida' meda' padi nya'. | They see that unhusked rice. |
| Sida' meda' engkayu' nya'. | They see that food. |
| Sida' meda' anak indu' nya'. | They see those girls. |
| Sida meda' anak lelaki nya'. | They see those boys. |
| Sida meda' Iban nya'. | They see that Iban. |
| Sida' meda' umai nya'. | They see that farm. |
| Sida' meda' manuk nya'. | They see that chicken. |
| Sida' meda' tikai nya'. | They see that mat. |
| | |
| Kati nuan makai manuk? | Do you eat chicken? |
| Kati iya makai manuk? | Does he or she eat chicken? |
| Kati kita makai manuk? | Do you eat chicken? |
| Kati sida' makai manuk? | Do they eat chicken? |
| Kati de' makai manuk? | Do you eat chicken? |
| Kati kita' makai uduk? | Do you eat dog? |
| Kati kita' makai engkayu'? | Do you eat food with your rice? |
| Kati kita' makai padi? | Do you eat unhusked rice? |

## Translate the following into English

Tikai aku di rumah apai.
Tikai nuan besai. Tikai aku mit.
Dini tikai kita'?
Sapa ngaga' tikai mit tu'?
Iban ngaga' rumah besai.
Kereja umai enggau kereja kampung, nya' meh pengindup Iban.
Di kampung nadai rumah.
Umai Iban umai padi.
Kitai makai manuk. Manuk makai padi.
Anak Penghulu pandai ngaga' rumah.
Ruai enggau bilik sida' sigi' badas.

## Translate the following into Iban.

Where is your father's house?
My wife is good at making mats.
My children know their lessons.
We are sleeping on your mats.
The dogs are sleeping under father's mat.
Your chickens ate my unhusked rice just now.
We are sitting on the mats eating chicken.
She is making mats at her mother's farm.
We eat jungle food, you eat town food.
My children are clever. They make good farms.

## Answer the following in Iban.

Kati bisi' mayuh tikai di rumah Iban?
Kati samua tikai nya' besai?
Sapa pandai ngaga' tikai?
Sida' Iban makai nama?
Dini rumah sida' Iban?
Dini Iban tinduk?
Nama kereja sida' Iban?
Iban pandai ngaga' nama?
Dini sida' Iban makai?
Kati nuan makai manuk?

| | | |
|---|---|---|
| | katas | (to) above, up |
| | anang | do not (imperative) |

| | |
|---|---|
| Katas, wai. | Up, above, friend. |
| Anang duduk di baruh. | Don't sit down below. |

| | | |
|---|---|---|
| | empai | Not yet |
| | chara | custom, manner, tradition |
| | patut | should, ought; proper; fitting |
| | ngajar | to teach, advise, warn |

| | |
|---|---|
| Aku empai nemu chara Iban, wai. | I do not yet know Iban manners, friend. |
| Patut nuan ngajar aku. | You must (i.e. should) teach me. |

| | | |
|---|---|---|
| | nemuai | to visit |
| | kitu' | (to) here, to this place, come here! |
| | datas | (at) above, on top. |
| | dia | there, at that place |

| | |
|---|---|
| Nuan nemuai kitu'. | You are visiting here. |
| Nuan duduk datas, dia'. | You sit up above, there. |

| | | |
|---|---|---|
| | baka | like, similar to |

| | |
|---|---|
| Au' duduk meh aku. | All right, I'm sitting. |
| Nyamai duduk baka tu'. | It is pleasant to sit like this. |

| | | |
|---|---|---|
| | asi' | cooked (boiled) rice |
| | ngena' | to use, wear, hit |
| | jari | hand |
| | enda' | not, no |
| | sudu' | spoon |

| | |
|---|---|
| Kami tu makai asi ngena' jari. | We eat rice with our hands. |
| Enda' nyamai makai asi' ngena' sudu'. | It is not tasty to eat rice with a spoon. |
| Nama engkayu', indai? | What is there to eat, mother? |

| | | |
|---|---|---|
| | babi | pig, pork |
| | ikan | fish |
| | tang | but |
| | ngasu | to hunting with the help of dogs |
| | nginti' | to fish with hook and line |

---

| | |
|---|---|
| Engkayu' babi. | A pork dish (i.e. food—pig). |
| Nadai ikan. | There is no fish. |
| Patut bisi' ikan. | There should be fish. |
| Tang anak ngasu tadi', enda' nginti'. | But son went hunting just now, not fishing. |

| | | |
|---|---|---|
| | dulu | (at) upriver |

| | |
|---|---|
| Dini anak ngasu? Dulu? | Where did son go hunting? Upriver? |

| | | |
|---|---|---|
| | dili' | (at) downriver |
| | ukai | is not, are not (any time: present, past, or future) |
| | ku' | to say, says, said (a contraction of jaku.") |
| | lubah | slowly |

| | |
|---|---|
| Dili'. Ukai dulu. | Downriver. Not upriver. |
| Ku' iya, nadai utai dulu. | He said there was nothing upriver. |
| Lubah makai, wai. | Eat slowly, friend. |
| Lubah makai. | Eat slowly. |

| | |
|---|---|
| anang enda' | must |
| kenyang | full, satisfied (of the stomach) |
| ditu' | here, at this place |
| taun | year |
| umbas | enough, sufficient |
| agi' | still; more |
| dumai | at the farm, at the rice field |
| angku | to carry (in successive loads) |

| | |
|---|---|
| Anang enda' makai kenyang, wai. | You must eat to the full, friend. |
| Mayuh asi' ditu'. | There is much rice here. |
| Padi kami taun tu' sigi' umbas. | Our rice (harvest) this year was sufficient. |
| Agi' bisi' mayuh padi kami dumai, emapi angkut. | There is still much of our rice at the farm, not yet carried (home). |

| | |
|---|---|
| bendar | truly, really, very |
| tau' | can, be able, may |
| enda' tau' enda' | must, it is necessary |
| orang | person, someone, anyone, people |

Asi' engkayu' tu' sigi' nyamai bendar.

The rice and other food are certainly very delicious.

Enda' tau' enda' orang makai kenyang.

Anyone would have to eat his fill.

## NOTE A: NEGATIVE

"Enda'"—"not"—before any word used as a verb, adverb or adjective is the simple negation of that word. Learn to use this construction. It is the most common form of the negative.

Indu' enda' ngasu.

Women do not hunt with dogs.

Tuai Rumah enda' makai tadi'.

The Tuai Rumah did not eat just now.

Penghulu enda' nemuai kulu tadi'.

The Penghulu did not visit upriver just now.

Tikai nya' enda' badas.

The mat is no good.

Engkayu' tu' enda' nyamai.

This food is not tasty.

"Empai"—"not yet"—is also a frequently used negative. It is usually placed in a sentence just before the verb, adverb or adjective it negates. It is used to indicate that at present a "not," or "no," is in order, but in the future this might be changed.

In English we frequently do not distinguish between the flat "not," and the more tentative "not yet." We tend to group everything under "not," or "no," The Ibans are much more careful to use "not yet" where it is applicable.

Sida' indu' empai' ngaga' tikai.

The women have not yet made mats.

Apai empai ngasu.

Father has not yet gone hunting.

Mayuh orang empai tinduk.

Many people are not yet asleep.

Kati nuan nemu pelajar tu'?

Do you know this lesson?

Empai.

No. (i.e. not yet)

Kati anak indu' nya' pandai ngaga tikai?

Are those girls good at making mats?

Empai.

No (i.e. not yet)

Nuan bisi' anak?

Do you have any children?

Empai.

No (i.e. not yet)

Where the predicate is an adjective or adverb, this predicate with its attached negative may be placed before the subject. This is done when you wish to emphasize the condition expressed by adjective or adverb.

Enda' besai rumah kami.

Our house is not large.

Empai angkut padi sida'.

There (unhusked) rice is not yet carried home.

("angkut" here is the equivalent of a participle used as an adjective.)

Empai kenyang aku.
I am not yet full (satisfied).

Enda' pandai indu' nya.
That woman is not skilled.

"Ukai" means "is not, are not." It is often used as an ordinary verb, with a subject.

Nya' ukai Penghulu.
This is not the Penghulu.

Tu' ukai manuk aku.
These are not my chickens.

Padi tu' ukai padi kita'.
This (unhusked) rice is not yours.

Indu' nya' ukai bini Tuai Rumah.
That woman is not the wife of the Tuai Rumah.

Ukai aku.
Not I! (It was not I!).

"Anang" is the negative command: "do not." It is used much like its English equivalent.

Anang tinduk di ruai.
Do not sleep on the veranda.

Anang ngaga' tikai besai.
Don't make a large mat.

Anang nuan nginti' dulu.
Don't you go fishing upriver?

Anang ka pasar.
Don't go to town.

Empai bisi' mayuh orang dia'.
There are not many people there yet.

## NOTE B. "MUST"—DOUBLE NEGATIVE

The double negatives, "anang enda'" and "enda' tau' enda'" are the commonly used expressions for "must," "have to," "it is necessary."

"Anang enda'" is the command: "must." It is usually used in the second person: "you must." Less frequently, it is used with the first or third person.

Used without a specific pronoun or other subject, "anang enda'" means "you must." The use of the second person pronoun makes the sentence more formal, or polite.

If the third person is intended, a pronoun or other subject must be specified.

Anang enda' ngajar aku.
You must teach me.

This form is more forceful than, "Patut nuan ngajar aku."

Anang enda' makai kenyang, wai.
You must eat to the full, friend.

Anang enda' nuan nemuai ka rumah, aku, Penghulu.
You must visit my house, Penghulu.

Anang enda' kita' nginti' dili.
You must fish downriver.

Anang enda' sida' ngaga rumah baru.
They must make a new house.

Anang enda' kitai makai asi' mayuh.
We must eat much rice.

Anang enda' iya nemuai kitu'.
He must visit here.

44

"Enda' tau' enda'," meaning "must," or "it is necessary," can be used with any pronount or noun. It is more forceful than "anang enda'," When you use "enda' tau' enda'" to a person to whom you are speaking, you are being quite peremptory with him or her.

| | |
|---|---|
| Enda' tau enda' kami Iban nemu kereja kampung enggau kereja umai. | It is necessary that we Ibans know the work of jungle and rice field. |
| Anak mit enda' tau' enda tinduk di bilik. | Little children must sleep in the room. |
| Kitu', de'. | Come here, you! |
| Enda' tau' enda' de ngaga' tikai baru. | You must make a new mat. |
| Sida' lelaki enda' tau' enda' ngasu, nginti'. | The Men must hunt and fish. |

## NOTE: C. ELISION OF FINAL VOWELS

Ibans, in conversation, commonly drop the final vowels of "di" and "ka" when these words immeditely precede a word beginning with a vowel. In written Iban some of these elisions are noted by joining the "d" or "k" directly to the following word, with no indication that basically two separate words, or ideas, are involved.

"Di" before a word not a verb means "at, in, on, by." Before a word beginning with a vowel, the "i" may be dropped, and the "d" joined directly to the word.

| | |
|---|---|
| dulu | at upriver |
| datas | at above |
| dili' | at downriver |

In English the above phrases are often merely "upriver," "above," "downriver;" and the context will inform you whether the speaker is talking about being "at" there, or proceeding "to" there. In Iban you should specify.

"Dumai," likewise, is often spoken by Ibans—though this form is seldom written. As your vocabulary increases you will note many more examples of the dropping of the "i" from "di"

"Ka" means among other things, "to, towards." With this meaning, when "ka" precedes a word beginning with a vowel, the "a" is often dropped, and the "k" is joined directly to the word.

| | |
|---|---|
| kulu | to upriver |
| katas | to above |
| kili' | to downriver |

Here also your increasing vocabulary will bring you more examples of this dropping of the "a" from "ka."

| | |
|---|---|
| Aku dulu. | I am upriver. |
| Aku kulu. | I am going upriver. |
| Bini iya dili'. | His wife is downriver. |
| Bini iya kili'. | His wife is going downriver. |
| Anak lelaki tinduk datas. | The boys sleep up above. |
| Tu' rumah kami. | This is our house. |
| Katas meh kitai, wai. | Up we go friends. |

## NOTE D. PRONUNCIATION OF "e"

Your teacher has been giving you the proper pronunciation of the words used in these lessons. Check with him or her concerning the sound that is written as "e" in syllables other than the final syllable of Iban words.

You will note that this is much like the sound of the unaccented "e" (or "a") in many English words—like the "e" in "churches," "loses."

In many cases—such as in "berapa"—the "e" is the barest minimal sound between two consonants.

Practice pronouncing the following words.

| | |
|---|---|
| besai | pelajar |
| meda' | berapa |
| nemu | penghulu |
| meri' | lelaki |
| ngena' | kereja |
| kenyang | pengidup |
| bendar | keresa |
| nemuai | engkayu' |
| enggau | empai |
| enda' | |

| | |
|---|---|
| Berapa iku' kita' anak lelaki empai nemu pelajar tu'? | How many of you boys do not yet know this lesson? |
| Penghulu besai meri' engkayu' nyamai. | The great Penghulu gives delicious food. |
| Mayuh orang empai meda' keresa Iban bendar. | Many people have not seen real Iban equipment. |

When the "e" is part of tjhe last, or only, syllable of an Iban word, then its sound is more nearly like that of the "e" in the English word "they." The latter English sound, however, is a diphthong (a combination of two vowel sounds); the Iban "e" is a single, pure vowel.

Your teacher will give you the pronunciations of the two words we have had so far in which there is an "e" as the only syllable.

di'
meh

Then note that the vowel sound in these two words is pronounced by many Ibans in nearly the same way that they pronounce the final vowels of the following words.

asi'    bisi'    tadi'
ili'    tabi'    dili'
sigi'   meri'    nginti'
agi'

| | |
|---|---|
| Kati de; makai asi' dili' tadi'? | Did you eat rice downriver just now? |
| Sigi' bisi' asi' tadi' dili'. | There truly was rice downriver just now. |
| Agi' bisi' lelaki nginti'. | There still are men fishing downriver. |
| Tabi', bini Ali. | Hello, wife of Ali. |
| Dini nginti' sida lelaki? | Where are the men fishing? |
| Ali meri' padi tadi'. | Ali gave unhusked rice just now. |
| Kami agi' bisi'. | We still have some. |

## NOTE E. WORDS AND PHRASES

"Duduk di baruh;" varioius parts of an Iban longhouse are termed "atas," or "baruh." When you meet your hosts on the "tanju'," or open veranda, they will possibly invite you "ka baruh."—meaning to come on inside the covered veranda or "ruai."

On the "ruai," the raised bench-like sitting place against the wall separating the "ruai" from the "tanju'" is considered a more honorable (or polite) place to sit. This is termed "atas." Honored guests, invited guests, are expected to sit here. The area before this sitting place, and especially the general walk-way bordering this area, are termed "baruh."

In the old-style Iban family rooms, the area around the hearth, or "dapur," is "baruh." The area away from this, where the beds are unrolled at night, is termed "atas." A guest in the room is expected to sit in the latter portion.

"Asi' engkayu';" boiled rice is the staple food of the Ibans. No eating experience is a true meal unless it includes "asi'." "Engkayu'" is a term which includes anything else eaten with the rice; vegetables, fish, meat, fruit or anything else. (Many Ibans these days are using the term "lauk" instead of "engkayu'."

"Makai asi'" is a phrase meaning not only "eat rice," but also "have a meal." A more extended phrase meaning to have a full meal is "makai asi' engkayu'."

"Lubah makai:" "eat slowly"—is a polite exhortation of host to guest. It means not only "eat slowly," but has the connotation: "eat slowly and eat to your fill."

"Makai kenyang" is the polite term meaning to eat to the full. To say that you are kenyang is the polite way of saying you have eaten all you can, you are full.

## EXERCISES

### Translate the following into English.

Anak tinduk di ruai.
Sapa ka pasar?
Kami empai nemu chara sida' Iban dulu.
Aku empai makai asi'.
Ikan tu' nyamai bendar.
Apai nginti' tadi' tang nadai ikan.
Anang enda' ngaga' tikai badas, anak.
Uduk enda' nemu ngaga' rumah.
Kati mayuh padi kita' taun tu'?
Apai enda' tau' enda' enggau anak ka pasar.

### Translate the following into Iban.

Do not eat my rice.
I must go downriver.
I have not yet seen Penghulu Sibat.
These children do not know their lesson yet.
Where is your mother?
My son must make a new house.
We cannot see the chickens.
He does not know how to make good mats.
You must make a visit to my house.
Does he know how to make good mats?

## Answer the following in Iban

Sapa nemu chara kampung?
Kati  nuan nemu nginti'?
Sida' Iban makai nama?
Kati nyamai engkayu' ikan?
Dini sida' Iban ngasu?

| | | |
|---|---|---|
| | ulih | Can, be able, possible |

| | |
|---|---|
| Kenyang aku, wai. | I am full, friend. |
| Enda ulih' makai agi'. | I can't eat any more. |
| Nyamai bendar asi' Iban. | Iban rice is very delicious. |

| | |
|---|---|
| gaga | glad, happy, pleased, joyful |
| ati | heart (as the seat of emotions) |
| sa | one—used in conjunction with other words; also expresses the idea of unity, or equality—in conjunction with other words. |

| | |
|---|---|
| sabilik | of one room, a family |
| diatu' | now, at this time (with the connotation of this moment, rather than period or era) |

| | |
|---|---|
| Tua | we two (i.e. you and I) |

| | |
|---|---|
| Gaga ati kami sabilik meda' nuan makai kenyang. | We of the family are happy to see you eat to the full. |
| Diatu', am tua ka ruai. | Now let's go to the veranda. |

| | |
|---|---|
| kabuah | reason, purpose |
| nama kabuah? | why? |
| berandau | to converse, chat, talk together |

| | |
|---|---|
| Nama kabuah enda' duduk berandau di bilik tu'? | Why not sit and talk in this room? |

| | |
|---|---|
| laban | because |
| enti' | if |
| niki' | to climb, ascend, go up |
| ngagai | to, towards; proceed to, go to, come to |
| ka' | to want, wish, will, like, desire |
| begulai | (intrans.) to mix together, associate |
| bala | group, band, troop, army, multitude, congregation |

Laban nya' ukai chara kami Iban.
That is not our Iban custom.

Enti' orang niki' rumah Iban, sida' indu' ngagai bilik, ka begulai enggau sida' bala indu' dia'.
If people go up into an Iban house, the women go to the room, to mix with the group of women there.

Sida' lelaki duduk di ruai, ka' begulai enggau bala lelaki.
The men sit on the veranda, to mix with the group of men.

| lebuh | when, at the time; in the midst |
| sagulai | associated or mixed together in one group (i.e. one mixture) |

Tang lebuh makai samua sagulai di bilik.
But when eating, all are together in this room.

| pia' | thus, like this, in this manner |
| pengawa' | concern, affair, business, work |
| enggai | will not, do not want, refuse |
| tama' | enter, go in, come in |

Au', pia' meh.
Yes, that's it.

Enti' nadai pengawa', lelaki enggai tama' bilik orang.
If there is no buisness (to call him in), a man will not go into someone else's room.

Tang enti' bisi' pengawa', sigi' tau' tama'.
But if there is some concern (to call him in), certainly he may enter.

| ngasuh | to order, command, tell, permit, allow; to cause to be; to send (a person) |

Nama pengawa' tau' ngasuh lelaki tama' bilik?
What business would cause a man to enter a room?

| empu | a word used following a noun or pronoun to show possession; to possess, own |

| nunda' | to follow, imitate |
| ka | a participle used after certain words to help complete their meaning. |

52

| | |
|---|---|
| nunda' ka | according to, in response |
| peneka' | a desire, wish, intention |

Lelaki sigi' tau' tama' bilik iya empu, nunda' ka peneka' ati iya.

A man may, of course, enter his own room according to his desire (i.e. whenever he wishes).

Tang enda' patut tama' bilik orang enti' sida iya enda' ngasuh.

But it is not right to enter the room of other people if they do not give permission.

| | |
|---|---|
| ila' | afterwards, in the future, subsequently |
| baru | recently, just, again |
| ngambi' ka | so that, in order that |

Ila' aku ka' kitu' baru, ngambi' ka nuan tau' ngajar aku.

Afterwards I wish to come here again so that you can teach me.

Diatu' mayuh pengawa' aku empai nemu.

Now there are many things I do not yet know.

| | |
|---|---|
| lagi' | presently, later on |
| undur | to proceed downriver' |
| kili' | (to) downriver |
| udah | finished, done; a word indicating finished or completed action |

Lagi' nuan duduk berandau di ruai, Iban sigi ngajar.

Presently you sit and talk on the veranda, and the Ibans truly will teach you.

Ila', undur kili', udah nemu, nuan.

Afterwards, when you go down river, you will have the knowledge (i.e. you will have known).

| | |
|---|---|
| pagi | morning |
| pagila' | tomorrow |
| minta' | to ask for, request (i.e. to ask for something, not to ask a question) |
| siku' | one—of any living creature |

Pagi pagila' aku ka' mupuk.

Tomorrow morning I shall start off.

Lalu ka' mina' siku' enggau aku kili', enti' ulih.

And I should like to ask for one man to accompany me downriver, if possible.

## NOTE A: VERB GROUPS

In Iban, two or more words used as verbs may be placed together in a verb group. Following are some examples.

|  |  |
|---|---|
| ka' | wish, want, desire, will, going to |

Apai ka' duduk.                                  Father wants to sit down.
Apai ka' makai.                                  Father wants to eat.
Apai ka' nginti' pagila'.                     Father will go fishing tomorrow.
Apai ka' berandau enggau sida' lagi'.    Father is going to talk with them later.

|  |  |
|---|---|
| tau' | can, be able, may |

Anak aku tau' meda' orang.          My child can see someone.
Anak aku tau' ngaga' pintu.        My child can make a door.
Anak aku tau' begulai enggau sida nya'.  My child may associate with them.

|  |  |
|---|---|
| bisi' | is, are |
| nemu | know how |
| ulih | can, be able |

Iban bisi' duduk di ruai.            Ibans are sitting on the veranda.
Penghulu bisi' nemuai' kili'.       The Penghulu is visiting downriver.
Anak iya nemu ngasu.              His son knows how to hunt with dogs.
Indai sida' nemu ngajar sida'.      Their mother knows how to teach them.

Bini aku enda' ulih undur pagila'.    My wife cannot go downriver tomorrow.

Sida' iya enda' ulih niki rumah kami.  They cannot come up into our house.

Another type of Iban verb group is a sequence of two or more words used as verbs, any two of which might, in the English version, be separated by "and."

Orang duduk berandau diatu'.       Folks are sitting and talking now.
Kami sabilik duduk makai          Our family is sitting and talking.
Tuai Rumah undur nemuai kili'.     The Tuai Rumah is going visiting downriver.

Here is a pair of verbs which you will occasionally see or hear together.

|  |  |
|---|---|
| nadai; bisi' | There are not; there are |

Nadai bisi' Iban di rumah.        There is not an Iban in the house. (i.e. There is no one at the house.)

| | |
|---|---|
| Aku nadai bisi' anak. | I do not have children. (i.e. I have no children.) |
| Sigi' nadai bisi' uduk dumai. | There certainly are no dogs at the farm. |

You have already seen how words indicating the negative are used with verbs.

| | |
|---|---|
| Kami sabilik nadai nemuai kili' taun tu'. | Our family has not visited downriver this year. |
| Bini aku enggai tinduk di ruai. | My wife will not sleep on the veranda. |
| Ku' iya, anang niki' rumah nya'. | Said he, don't go up into that house. |

The terms expressing command, or necessity, also make up verb groups.

| | |
|---|---|
| Anang enda' undur kitu' ila'. | You must come downriver here later. |
| Sida' lelaki enda' tau' enda' nginti' pagila. | The men must go fishing tomorrow. |

Then there are words which do not look like verbs from the English point of view, but which, in Iban, are used as verbs. These can make other verb groups.

| | |
|---|---|
| kitu' | Come here |
| Kili' | go (come) downriver |
| katas | go (come) up |

| | |
|---|---|
| Aku ka' kitu' baru ila'. | I want to come here again afterwards. |
| Nuan enda' tau' enda' kili' niki' rumah Penghulu. | You must go downriver and visit the Penghulu's house. |
| Anak nya' ka' katas meda' indai iya. | That child wants to go up and see his mother |

## NOTE B. USE OF "SA"

"Sa" is the word meaning "one." It is used, however, only in combination with other words.

When counting, or when using "one" as a simple numeral by itself, as in arithmetic, the form "satu" is used.

"Sa" is added as a prefix to the word it modifies. Before a consonant, the "sa-" keeps its full form. It is generally, however, pronounced "se-". Because of this prnounciation, some words with this prefix use the spelling "se-."

When "sa-" is attached to a numeral classifier which begins with a vowel, the "a" is commonly dropped—as in "siku'" (from "sa—iku'"). When "sa-" is attached to a word of measurement, or to a noun or adjective which begins with a vowel, the combination is written as a hyphenated word—as in "sa-ati."

## "Sa-" — "one"

The prefix "sa-," meaning "one," is attached to numeral classifiers (See Note B: Lesson 2), and to words of amount or measurement.

| | |
|---|---|
| siku' | one—of any living creature. |
| sigi' | one—of eggs, fruit, or other similarly small objects. |
| sapuluh | ten (i.e. one ten) |
| sataun | one year |
| sasudu' | one spoonful |

| | |
|---|---|
| Aku bisi' siku' babi. | I have one pig. |
| Uduk aku tiga iku'. | I have three dogs. |
| Dua iku' di rumah. | Two are at the house. |
| Siku' dumai. | One is at the farm. |
| Kati, bisi' Iban di rumah? | Are there Ibans at the house? |
| Au', bisi'—siku'. | Yes, there is—one. |
| Nadai anak di bilik kami. | There are no children in our room. |
| Siku' nadai. | There is not even one. |
| Indu' siku' undur kili' tadi'. | One woman went downriver just now. |
| Indai aku bisi' sapuluh iku' manuk. | My mother has ten chickens. |
| Rumah sida' nya' enda' besai. | Their house is not large. |
| Bisi' sapuluh pintu. | There are ten doors. (i.e. rooms). |
| Berapa taun kita lelaki dili'? | How many years were you downriver? |
| Kami sataun dili'. | We were downriver one year. |
| Anak aku enggai makai tadi'. | My child refused to eat just now. |
| Sasudu' asi' enggai'. | One spoonful of rice he would not eat. |

## "Sa" — the idea of unity

"Sa-" expresses the idea of unity: when used as a prefix for any noun which is other than a numeral classifier or a word denoting amount or measure.

Following are some of the words we have already had which may be used with this construction.

| | |
|---|---|
| sabilik | of one room—i.e. family |
| sarumah | of one house (from the same house) |
| sapasar | of one village (from the same village) |

| | |
|---|---|
| sa-apai | having one (the same) father |
| sa-indai | having one (the same) mother |
| sachara | of one custom, or tradition |
| sa-ati | of one mind (this is a common word meaning being in agreement about anything) |
| sagulai | of one mixture (this is a common word meaning all together) |

| | |
|---|---|
| Sida' sabilik nadai padi taun tu'. | That (their) family has no rice this year. |
| Kami sarumah bisi' umbas padi taun tu'. | We of our house have enough rice this year. |
| Sida' tiga iku' sapasar enggau kami. | These three are from the same village that we are. |
| Indu' nya' lima' iku' sigi' sa-apai. | These five women have the same father. |
| Bisi' dua iku' anak dulu, lima' iku' dili'; tang samua nya' bendar sa-indai. | There are two children upriver, and five downriver; but they all really have the same mother. |
| Samua kami Iban dulu sigi' sachara. | All of us Ibans upriver have the same customs. |
| Samua sida' ari rumah nya' sigi' sa-ati—ka' undur ka pasar pagila'. | All these from that house are of one mind—they wish to go down to the village tomorrow. |
| Enti' kita' sa-ati—ka' undur ka pasar pagila'. | If you are of the same mind with us you must come here tomorrow. |
| Samua sida duduk sagulai di ruai. | They all sat together on the veranda. |

## "Sa-" — the idea of equality

"Sa-"—as a prefix to adjectives and adverbs, indicates equality.

| | |
|---|---|
| sabesai | as big |
| samayuh | as many |
| sapandai | as clever |
| satuai | as old |

| | |
|---|---|
| Rumah kami sabesai enggau rumah Penghulu. | Our house is as big as the Penghulu's house. |
| Manuk aku samayuh enggau manuk de'. | I have as many chickens as you. (i.e. My chickens are as numerous as your chickens). |

Anak indu' sigi' sapandai enggau anak lelaki.
Apai nuan satuai enggau apai aku.

Girls are truly just as clever as boys.
Your father is as old as my father.

## NOTE C: WORDS AND PHRASES

1. "Ulih" has two important meanings. The one we are using in this lesson is the idea of being able, it being possible. (The other meaning: "to get, obtain.") This is expressed by the English "can," or "be able." This word, then, must be distinguished from the word "tau'." "Tau'" means both "can" and "may." "Ulih" means "can."

2. "Ati" metaphorically means "heart." Anatomically it means "liver." The various emotions are described in Iban usually with some phrase using the word "ati." In the openiing sentences of this lesson one such phrase is used—"gaga ati"— meaning "glad, happy, joyful, pleased." Some of the other adjectives we have had may also be linked with the word "ati" to describe an emotion or feeling.

| | |
|---|---|
| gaga ati | glad, happy, joyful, pleased |
| besai ati | proud (in the bad sense of the word), overbearing, condescending |
| baruh ati | humble, meek |
| badas ati | kind, generous, good-hearted |

Gaga ati Penghulu Iban mayuh orang nemuai ka rumah iya.

The Penghulu is glad because many people are visiting his house.

Besai ati Tuai Rumah nya', laban iya mayuh bendar.

That Tuai Rumah is proud because he has many possessions.

Tuai Rumah tu' ukai baka nya'.

This Tuai Rumah is not like that.

Utai iya tu' mayuh bendar, tang iya sigi' baruh ati.

He has a great many possessions, but he is truly humble of heart.

Sigi' badas ati bini Penghulu.

The wife of the Penghulu is really kind and generous.

Iya ngasuh samua anak nya' makai kenyang.

She is making alll those children eat to the full.

3. The phrase "peneka' ati iya" means the "desire of the heart." But the Iban does not carry the connotation of intensity of desire that the equivalent English phrase has. The Iban simply means, whatever desire he or she may happen to have in his or her heart or mind.

4. "Tua" is the last of the Iban pronouns. Meaning "we two," it is used by a speaker when talking to one other person, and includes the speaker and the person to whom he or she is talking. Another word would have to be used to indicate any pair other than these two.

5. "Niki' rumah" has come to mean the entering or the visiting of almost any house or building, though the origin of the phrase is rooted in the fact that the Iban longhouse is built on tall posts. To get into the traditional Iban longhouse, a person had literally to "climb up" into the house.

6. "Orang" is a word of vaguely defined meanings. It can mean "person," or "someone" or "somebody else." It is often translated as "man"—in the sense of a person or individual.

| | |
|---|---|
| Kati, mayuh orang di pasar tadi'? | Were there many people in town just now. |
| Au', mayuh bendar orang dia'. | Yes, a great many people were there. |
| Enti' orang ka' niki' rumah Iban, tau' meh. | If someone wants to enter an Iban house, he or she may. |

The word "orang" is frequently used in phrases which look like "somebody," or "somebody's so and so," but have the very clear connotation of "somebody else," or "somebody else's so and so."

| | |
|---|---|
| Tu' bilik aku. Nya' bilik orang. | This is my room. That is somebody else's room. |
| Anang ngasuh anak nuan makai engkayu' orang. | Do not permit your children to eat some other person's food. |
| Uduk kita' udah makai manuk orang. | Your dog has eaten someone else's chicken. |

"Ila'" and "lagi'" mean "afterwards, later on," but they have different usages. "Ila'" means afterwards in the sense of a time after today; whether it be tomorrow, or next week or a year or more from now. "lagi'" (often "nagi'") means afterwards or later on —but in this same day. It is later on today.

"Kili'" and "siku'" are two further examples of elision met in this lesson. "Kili'" is the abbreviation of "ka—ili'," meaning "to downriver." "Siku'" is the abbreviation of "sa—iku'," meaning "one tail"—that is, "one" of any living creature.

"Pengawa'" is a general-purpose word which can be translated in a number of ways. Built up from the root "gawa'," it means, strictly, "what is done." In various contexts it is so used as to be translatable as: "business, work, affair, matter, concern, thing."

"Ka'," meaning "to desire, want, wish, like," is also used in conjunction with other verbs to indicate the simple future tense.

| | |
|---|---|
| Pagila' Penghulu ka' undur kili'. | Tomorrow the Penghulu will go downriver. |
| Kami sabilik ka' makai lagi'. | Our family will eat later. |

Diatu' kitai berandau di ruai.

Now we are talking together on the veranda.

Lagi' ka' tinduk di bilik.

Later we shall sleep in the room.

"Baru" originally means "new." Used as an adverb, it means "anew, again," or "newly, just"—depending on its position in relation to the verb it conditions. Following the verb, it means "anew, again."

Pagila' kami ka' undur baru.

Tomorrow we shall go downriver again.

Lagi' samua kitai tau' begulai baru.

Later we can all get together again.

Tadi' aku ngajar sida' baru.

Just now I warned them again.

Ordinarily there should be no more than one word separating the verb from the adverb "baru" which conditions it. Preceding the verb, "baru" means "newly, just."

Sida' iya baru undur.

They have just gone downriver.

Kitai tu' baru begulai.

We have just got together.

Aku baru ngajar sida'.

I am just warning them.

"Udah" is the word indicating a completed action or condition—in any time setting: past, present or future.

Tuai Rumah udah meri' iya manuk siku'.

The Tuai Rumah has given him a chicken.

Udah diangkut, padi kami.

Our rice (harvest) has already been carried home.

Pagila' samua sida' Penghulu ka' berandau, udah begulai.

Tomorrow all the Pengulus will talk together, if they have already' gathered together.

Udah nginti' kami tadi'.

We had fished just now.

Udah besai, anak aku.

My child is already big.

Apai sida' udah tuai.

Their father is old.

Note that when a yes-or-no question is asked in which the main verb uses "udah," the answer, if in the affirmative, is commonly "udah."

Udah makai kita'? Udah.

Have you eaten? Yes. (i.e. we have)

Kati sida', udah undur? Udah.

Have they gone downriver? Yes.

Kati Penghulu udah niki' rumah nuan? Udah.

Has the Penghulu visited your house? Yes.

Kati indai sida' udah tuai? Udah.

Is their mother old? Yes.

| | bagi | division, section, chapter; to divide |
|---|---|---|
| | dai' | at the water, at the stream |
| | turun | to descend, go down, come down; go to work on the farm |
| | datai | to come, arrive |
| | ai' | water, stream, river |
| | perau' | boat, the longboat of the Ibans |

Am, turun kitai, wai, datai dia'. — Come, let's go down, friend, and get to the river.

Bisi' perau' dia'. — There are boats there.

| | (asuh | |
|---|---|---|
| | (ngasuh | to order, command, tell, permit, allow; to cause to be; to send a person |
| | (kayuh | |
| | (ngayuh | to paddle (a boat) |

Baka ni nuan ka' ngasuh aku kili'? — How are you going to send me down river?

Ka' ngayuh ka perau'? — Paddling a boat?

| | moto | motor, outboard motor |
|---|---|---|
| | (luan | |
| | (ngeluan | prow, front end of any boat or vehicle; to act as a prowsman |
| | (kemudi | |
| | (ngemudi | stern (of boat), rear end of any boat or vehicle, rudder; to steer (a boat) |

Ukai pia'. — Not like that.
Bisi' moto. — There is a motor.
Nuan duduk di perau'. — You sit in the boat.
Bisi' siku' ngeluan ka perau' nya'. — There will be one person to act as prowsman for the boat.
Bisi siku ngemudi. — There will be one person to steer.

| | tentu | certainly, surely, certain, sure |
|---|---|---|
| | sengayuh | a paddle |

Enti' pia', badas meh! — If that is the way, good!
Aku enda' tentu pandai ngena' sengayuh. — I am not very good at using a paddle.

| | | |
|---|---|---|
| | ke (ti') | who, which, that |

Sida' iya ke enggau nuan kili' sigi' pandai bendar.

Those who will accompany you downriver are really clever.

Nadai ke pandai agi'.

There are none more skillful.

| kaki | foot, leg, base |
|---|---|
| tangga' | ladder, stairs, steps, the notched log used as a ladder or stairs |
| buah | fruit, nut, berry; Numeral Classifier for houses, buildings, boats, ships, etc. |

Di kaki tangga' nya' bisi' tiga buah perau'.

At the foot of those steps there are three boats.

Kati sabuah nya' perau' kami?

Is one of them our boat?

| udu | very, exceedingly |
|---|---|
| mimit | a little, some, not much |
| ba' | at, in, on |

Ukai. Perau' tu' udu mit.

No. This boat is very small.

Dili' mimit bisi' perau' besai ari tu'.

Downriver a little there is a boat larger than this.

Nyamai bendar duduk ba' perau' nya'.

It is very comfortable to sit in that boat.

| din | there, at that place, yonder |
|---|---|
| kurang | less, fewer, lacking, insufficient |

Aku meda' sabuah perau' dili' din, tang perau' nya' kurang besai ari perau' tu'.

I see a boat downriver, there; but that boat is smaller than this boat.

| amat | true, right, truly verily |
|---|---|
| pemadu' | extremely, the furthest extent; the word forming the superlative degree of any adjective or adverb. |

Au', amat.

Yes, that's right.

Perau' nya' ke pemadu' besai.

That boat is the biggest.

| | |
|---|---|
| gaga' | |
| ngaga' | To make, construct, build, do, accomplish |

| | |
|---|---|
| Perau' nya' besai amat, tang perau' kami ke pemadu besai dulu. | That boat is quite large, but our largest boat is upriver. |
| Kami ka' ngaga baru luan iya. | We are planning to repair its prow. |
| Perau' tu' mit agi' ari perau' nya' dulu. | This boat is smaller than that boat upriver. |

| | |
|---|---|
| (ulih | |
| (ngulih | to obtain, get |
| takut | afraid, fearful; to fear |
| (rusak | |
| (ngerusak | to spoil, destroy, ruin; spoiled, ruined, out of commission, destroyed |
| (intu | |
| (ngintu | to care for, watch over, take care of |
| (mansang | |
| (ngemansang | to advance, develop, progress |

| | |
|---|---|
| Ila' aku ka' ngulih ka perau' baru. | Afterwards I want to get a new boat. |
| Ka' ngemansang ka kereja aku. | I want to develop my work. |
| Tang takut ngerusak ka perau' nya' laban empai tentu nemu ngintu iya. | But I'm afraid of spoiling that boat, because I don't know much about taking care of it. |

## NOTE A: NASAL PREFIXES TO VERBS

Many words in Iban have root forms which may be altered by the use of various prefixs or suffixes. The commonest of these changes is the nasal prefix added to words used as verbs. These changes occur for the most part, in regular fashion.

In this lesson we have seen and used the regular nasal prefix for words beginning with:

| | |
|---|---|
| asuh—ngasuh | (vowels) — a, e, i, u |
| intu—ngintu | |
| ulih—ngulih | |
| | |
| gaga'—ngaga' | g, k |
| kayuh—ngayuh | |
| kemudi—ngemudi | |

luan—ngeluan        l, m, r
mansang—ngemansang
rusak—ngerusak

- That is, words used as verbs, and beginning with a vowel, add the prefix "ng-."
- Words used as verbs, and beginning with "g" or "k," change the initial "g" or "k" to "ng-"
- Words used as verbs, and beginning with "l,", "m," "r," and sometimes "n" add the prefix "nge-."

A verb may take the nasal prefix:

- when a word used as a verb is used as though it were in the active voice rather than the passive;
- when a word is used as a verb, though its basic meaning in the root form is that of a noun, an adjective, an adverb, a preposition or a conjunction;
- when the meaning of a word used as a verb is such as to make possible the taking of an object—whether an object actually be present or not.

Always remember, too, that after translation a sentence, in its English form, may have an entirely different-appearing grammatical structure than that of the Iban original.

| | | |
|---|---|---|
| | ajar | teaching, advice, warning |
| | ngajar | to teach, advise, warn |

Sida' iya ngajar anak mit.                  They are teaching little children.

| | | |
|---|---|---|
| | ginti' | fish hook |
| | nginti' | to fish with hook and line |

Kami ka' undur pagila', ka' nginti' dili'.    We shall go downriver tomorrow to fish downriver.

| | | |
|---|---|---|
| | angkut | to carry (in successive loads) |
| | ngangkut | to carry (in successive loads) |

Sida' sabilik baru ngangkut padi.         That family is just now carrying home the rice.

| | | |
|---|---|---|
| | gaga' | to make, do, accomplish |
| | ngaga' | to make, do, accomplish |

Bini aku udah ngaga' tikai baru.          My wife has made a new mat.

| | | |
|---|---|---|
| | luan | prow |
| | ngeluan | to act as prowman |

| | |
|---|---|
| Sapa ka' ngeluan? | Who wants to be prowsman? |
| Aku ka' ngeluan. | I want to act as prowsman. |

| | | |
|---|---|---|
| | nyamai | happy, pleasant, comfortable, etc. |
| | ngenyamai | to please, make comfortable, etc. |

| | |
|---|---|
| Iya ngenyamai ka ati bini iya. | He pleased his wife. (i.e. He made happy the heart of his wife.) |

| | | |
|---|---|---|
| | asu | hunting with dogs |
| | ngasu | to hunt with dogs |

| | |
|---|---|
| Pagi tadi sida' tiga iku' lelaki meda' babi. | This morning the three men saw pigs. |
| Lagi' sida' ka' ngasu. | In a little while they will go hunting with the dogs. |

| | | |
|---|---|---|
| | rusak | spoiled, ruined, out of commission. |
| | ngerusak | to spoil, ruin, destroy |

| | |
|---|---|
| Anak enda' nemu ngintu moto. | Children don't know how to take care motors. |
| Sida' udah ngerusak ka moto tu'. | They have already ruined this motor. |

### A verb omits the nasal prefix:

**...when that verb is used in a command, and entreaty or an exhortation;**

| | |
|---|---|
| Ajar sida' anak mit. | Teach those little children |
| Ginti' dili', kita'. | Fish downriver. |
| Gaga' tikai baru. | Make a new mat. |
| Asuh anak nuan kitu'. | Tell (i.e. order) your child to come here. |
| Asu meh kitai. | Let's go hunting with the dogs. |
| Rusak ka perau' nya' ke enda' badas. | Destroy that boat that is no good. |

---

### ...when the verb is used as a past participial adjective—
### with or without an agent being specified;

(this construction is used when the root form of the word has the meaning of a verb)

| | |
|---|---|
| Samua padi nya' angkut kami tadi'. | All that rice was carried by us just now. |

(Normal English grammatical construction demands that "angkut" here be translated as "was carried.")

| | |
|---|---|
| Tikai baru tu' gaga' bini aku. | This new mat was made by my wife. |
| Sigi' gaga' badas bendar. | It is very well made. |
| Anak indu' nya' tinggal di ruai. | That girl was left on the veranda. |
| Mayuh ikan ulih sida' dulu. | Many fish were obtained by them upriver. |

### ...when that verb is used intransitively, and when in its root form
### it has the meaning of an intransitive verb;

| | |
|---|---|
| Sida' anak lelaki tinduk di ruai'. | The boys are sleeping on the veranda. |
| Bala orang mayuh duduk di ruai. | Many people are sitting on the veranda. |

### ...when, with certain words, the English translation gives a transitive verb in
### the indicative mood, but the Iban uses the root form of what is confusingly
### similar to both verb and adjective.

(We have not had examples of these yet, but the following may be mentioned;)

| | |
|---|---|
| deka' | to want, wish, like |
| rindu' | to love, be happy or pleased |
| sayau | to have pity or compassion |

### ...when the verb is used in the passive voice.

The passive voice has not been given in these lessons. A verb in the passive voice, however, takes a "di" prefix instead of the nasal prefix.)

Following is table of the changes involved in the use of the nasal prefix.

| Verb Beginning with: | Initial Letter Changed to: | Prefix Added: | Some Examples: | | |
|---|---|---|---|---|---|
| a, e, i, u | — | ng- | asuh | — | ngasuh |
| | | | empu | — | ngempu |
| | | | intu | — | ngintu |
| | | | ulih | — | Ngulih |
| l, r, m, (n) | — | nge | laban | — | ngelaban |
| | | | rusak | — | ngerusak |
| | | | malu | — | ngemalu |
| | | | nyamai | — | ngenyamai |
| g, k | ng | — | gaga' | — | ngaga; |
| | | | kena' | — | ngena' |
| d, t | n | — | dinga | — | ninga |
| | | | temu | — | nemu |
| b, p | m | — | beli | — | meli |
| | | | pinta' | — | minta' |
| ch, j, s | ny | — | chabut | — | nyabut |
| | | | jual | — | nyual |
| | | | sambut | — | nyambut |
| n | — | — | ngabang | — | ngabang |

In compiling lists of Iban words, editors give the root forms of verbs. So when you see an unfamiliar Iban verb with a nasal prefix, first decide what the root form might be, then look that up in your dictionary or word list.

| | |
|---|---|
| mupuk | to be looked up: "bupuk," "pupuk" |
| ngaga' | to be looked up: "aga'," "gaga'," "kaga'" |
| nemuai | to be looked up: "demuai," "temuai" |

## NOTE B: COMPARISON OF ADJECTIVES

1. A simple adjective takes no affix of any kind. Adjectives of number and quantity normally precede the substantives they modify. Other adjectives normally follow the substantive. For emphasis these normal positions may be reversed.

| | |
|---|---|
| Dili' bisi' mayuh rumah. | There are many houses downriver. |
| Bisi' rumah besai. | There are big houses. |
| Bisi' ga' rumah mit. | There are small houses. |
| Tu' Jaku' bendar. | This is a true saying. |
| Tiga iku' anak lelaki undur kili' tadi'. | Three boys went downriver just now. |
| Samua indu' nya nemu ngaga' tikai badas. | All those women know how to make good mats. |

2. A simple adjective may be modified by a number of words which either intensify or detract from the force of that adjective.

*Intensifiers:*

| | | |
|---|---|---|
| udu | very | —usually preceding the adjective |
| sigi' | really | —preceding the adjective |
| bendar | truly | —usually following the adjectives |
| amat | truly | —usually following the adjectives |
| pemadu' | uttermost | —preceding the adjectives |

| | |
|---|---|
| Udu besai rumah sida'. | Their house is very big. |
| Aku sigi' kenyang. | I am really full. |
| Apai aku tuai bendar. | My father is really old. |
| | (My father is very old.) |
| Apai Penghulu nya' sigi tuai bendar. | That Penghulu's father is really old. |
| Anak lelaki nya' pandai amat (amat pandai). | That boy is truly clever. |
| | (That boy is very clever.) |
| Pemadu' nyamai engkayu' tu'. | This food is extremely delicious. |

LESSON 6

*Detractors:*

| | |
|---|---|
| enda' tentu | Not certain, not very—preceding the adjective |
| kurang | less — — — preceding the adjective |

Perau' kami sabilik enda' tentu besai.
Aku kurang pandai nginti'.

Our family boat is not very large.
I am not very clever at fishing with a hook and line.

3. The comparative degree of an adjective is formed by using:

| | |
|---|---|
| agi' | more—following the adjective |
| lebih | more—preceding the adjective |
| kurang | less—preceding the adjective |

Rumah Penghulu besai agi' ari Rumah aku.

The Penghulu's house is bigger than my house.

(This is the usual, standard construction for the comparative degree. Frequently, however, this same type of construction is used without the "agi'," as follows.)

Apai nuan tuai ari apai aku.
Anak indu' aku lebih pandai ari anak lelaki aku.
Engkayu' manuk lebih nyamai agi' ari engkayu' ikan.
Jaku' orang nya' kurang tentu ari jaku' Penghulu

Your father is older than my father.
My daughter is more clever than my son.
A chicken dish is more delicious than a fish dish.
That man's word is less certain (i.e. less dependable) than the Penghulu's word.

4. The superlative degree of an adjective is formed by using:

| | |
|---|---|
| pemadu' | the uttermost—preceding the adjective. |
| pengambis | the end—preceding the adjective |

Di ai' tu' sigi' mayuh rumah besai.

In this river valley there are many large houses.

But the largest house, that is the Penghulu's house.
Engkayu' kami pemadu' nyamai.
Ikan ulih aku mit bendar.
Ikan ulih nuan mit agi'.
Tang ikan ke pengambis mit, nya' meh ikan ulih sida' anak nya'.

But the largest house, that is the Penghulu's house.
Our food is the most delicious.
The fish I obtained are quite small.
The fish you got are smaller.
But the smallest fish, those were the fish obtained by those children.

## NOTE C: WORDS AND PHRASES

"Ke" is the relative pronoun (who, which, that) most commonly used in the Kapit District of the Third Division, Sarawak. This corresponds to the "ti'" which is most commonly used in the Second Division. "Ti;" is the form used most extensively in the printed material of the Iban language.

"Ke" is an unstressed, single-syllable word. In the Third Division it is pronounced so as to rhyme with the English word "say."

"Sida' iya" is a colloquial phrase meaning simply "they." It is used frequently instead of the single word "sida'." It is used in positions where it is the subject of a verb, but not as the object of a verb.

| | |
|---|---|
| Bisi' mayuh Iban di rumah aku. | There are many Ibans at my house. |
| Sida' iya baru datai. | They have just come. |
| Lima' iku' anak Penghulu undur tadi. | Five children of the Penghulu went downriver just now. |
| Sida' iya' ngayuh ka perau' mit. | They paddled a small boat. |
| Sida' iya duduk di ruai, lalu berandau enggau Tuai Rumah. | They are sitting on the veranda and chatting with the Tuai Rumah. |

### *Numerical Classifiers: "buah," "tangga'"*

"Buah" is the numeral classifier for boats ("perau'" "kapal" etc.) houses ("rumah," "langkau," "kubu," etc.) hills and mountains ("bukit"), and other large, bulky things.

"Tangga'" is sometimes used as the numeral classifier for local-type wooden houses which are built up off the ground, and which are reached by climbing a ladder or steps.

| | |
|---|---|
| Bisi' dua puluh buah perau' dai'. | There are twenty boats at the river. |
| Di ai' mit tu' bisi' tiga buah rumah. | On this small stream there are three small houses. |
| Mayuh perau' undur ka pasar tadi, sabuah perau' ari sabuah rumah. | Many boats went down to the town just now, one boat from each house. |
| Moto aku rusak. Aku ka pasar ka' ngasuh orang ngaga baru. | My motor is out of commission. I am going to town to tell someone to repair it. |
| Rumah apai aku enda' badas. | My father's house is not good. |
| Iya ka' ngaga' baru ila'. | He is going to repair it later. |
| Pagila' kami ka' ngaga' baru ruai kami, laban rusak. | Tomorrow we shall repair our veranda, because it is in bad condition. |

# BIBLICAL TERMS

| | |
|---|---|
| Angel | Malikat |
| Christ | Almesih |
| Apostle | Rasul |
| Church | Eklesia |
| Demon | Antu |
| Disciple | Murid; Anembiak |
| Eternal Life | Pengidup ke Meruan |
| Evil Spirit | Roh ti jai |
| Forgive | Ampun |
| God | Allah Taala |
| god | Petara |
| Good news | Berita Manah |
| Gospel | Injil |
| Heaven | Serega |
| Hell | Naraka |
| Holy Spirit | Roh Alkudus, Roh Kudus |
| Image | Gamal |
| Jesus | Isa |
| Kingdom | Perintah |
| Lord | Tuhan |
| Offering | Piring |
| Pastor | Paderi |
| Priest | Imam |
| Prayer | Sampi |
| Prophet | Nabi |
| Resurrection | Angkat pulai idup ari mati |
| Satam | Sitan |
| Sin | Dosa |
| Spirit | Antu |
| Worship | Sembiang |

# OTHER BOOKS BY THE AUTHOR

## BIBLE STUDY GUIDES

1. **The Bible as Sacred History:**
Survey of the Whole Bible

2. **The Struggle with God:**
Genesis through Deuteronomy

3. **Sacred Stories:**
Joshua through Esther

4. **The Search for Wisdom:**
Job through Ecclesiastes

5. **Time is Running Out:**
Major and Minor Prophets

6. **Between the Testaments:**
Books of the Apocrypha

7. **The Messengers:**
The Four Gospels

8. **An Explosion of Faith:**
Acts and Revelation

9. **The First E-Letters:**
All of the Letters

10. **The Second Creation:**
Revelation (Formatted: 6x9)

11. **A Vision of Hope:**
Revelation: (Formatted 8.5x11)

12. **New Testament Photos 1**
The Gospels

13. **New Testament Photos 2**
The Letters

## BOOKS

1. **Ignited for Mission:**
A Call to Missions

2. **Reformulating the Mission of the Church:**
A Theology of Missions

3. **Our Spiritual Senses:**
Five Spiritual Senses

4. **Our Spiritual Disciplines:**
Six Spiritual Disciplines

5. **The Ordinary Christian Experience:**
Fourteen Ordinary Experiences

6. **Faith is a Choice:**
Choosing Faith and Morality

7. **A Brief Story of the Christian Church:**
A Survey of the Church

8. **The Heart of Methodism:**
Renewing the Church

9. **The Light**
Our Moral Compass

## EDITED

1. **Foundational Documents:**
Basic Methodist Documents

2. **Instructions for Children:**
by John Wesley

3. **Speaking Iban:**
by Burr Baughman

4. **The Essentials of Methodism:**
Basic Methodist Beliefs

Printed in Great Britain
by Amazon